DOUBLESPEAK:
Language for Sale

DOUBLESPEAK:
Language for Sale

William Sparke

Beatrice Taines

Diablo Valley College

Shirley Sidell

Photography Editor

Harper's College Press

A Department of Harper & Row, Publishers   New York   Evanston   San Francisco   London

Library of Congress Catalog Card Number: 74—3226

SBN: 06-160403-8

Produced by Kenneth R. Burke
Copyediting by Judith Fillmore
Design and art direction by Christine Butterfield
Composition by CBM Type
Printing by Kingsport Press

Credits for printed material

P. 1. Reprinted by permission of NCTE.

P. 7. Leo Rosten, from ''Movies and Propaganda,'' in *The Motion Picture Industry*, ed. Gordon S. Watkins, Annals of the American Academy of Political and Social Science, CCLIV (November 1947). Reprinted by permission of the American Academy of Political and Social Science.

P. 14. From Mario Savio's ''An End to History'' in *Humanity*, December, 1964.

P. 14. From Timothy Leary's ''American Education as an Addictive Process and it's Cure.'' Reprinted by permission of G. P. Putnam's Sons from *The Politics of Ecstasy by Timothy Leary.* Copyright © 1965, 1966, 1967, 1968 by The League for Spiritual Discovery, Inc.

P. 15. From Louis Kampf's ''The Humanities and Inhumanities.'' Reprinted by permission of *The Nation.*

P. 29. From ''Journalism and Truth,'' by Edward J. Epstein, *Commentary,* April 1974. Copyright © 1974 by the American Jewish Committee. Reprinted by permission.

P. 32. From Theodore H. White's *The Making of the President 1972.* Atheneum Publishers, New York, 1973.

P. 33. From *Prefaces* (1919), by Don Marquis. Copyright 1919, by D. Appleton and Company. Copyright, 1918, by the Sun Printing and Publishing Association. Reprinted by permission of Prentice-Hall, Inc.

P.38—39. From Harry Walker's *Modern Advertising: Practices & Principles,* 3rd ed., McGraw-Hill Book Company, New York, 1956.

P. 39. ''Our Kind of Advertising'' reprinted by permission of Foote, Cone, & Belding.

P. 40. From Walter A. Gaw's *Advertising: Methods and Media,* Wadsworth Publishing Co., Inc., San Francisco, 1961.

P. 41. From Philip Slater's *The Pursuit of Loneliness: American Culture at the Breaking Point,* Beacon Press, Boston, 1970.

P. 48. From ''Gobbledygookese'' by Russell Baker. Copyright © 1958 by The New York Times. Reprinted by permission.

P. 49. From ''Watergate Lingo: A Language of Non-Responsibility,'' by Richard Gambino, in *Freedom at Issue,* November/December, 1973. Reprinted by permission of Richard Gambino.

P. 59. ''Man Bites PG&E'' by Theodore Roszak, in *Co-op News* (weekly publication of consumers cooperative of Berkeley). Reprinted by permission.

P. 61. ''Home Buyers Guide,'' by Richard Lipez. Copyright 1973 by Harper's Magazine. Reprinted from the November 1973 issue by special permission.

P. 64. ''I Like the Word Forever,'' from *Thirty Two Love Poems* by Margaret Cesa. Copyright © 1973 by Margaret Cesa. Reprinted by permission.

P. 64. ''Canticle'' from *Hymns to St. Geryon and Other Poems* by Michael McClure. Copyright © 1959 by Michael McClure. Reprinted by permission.

P. 65. ''Poem,'' by Robin Blaser. Reprinted by permission.

P. 65. ''We Wear the Mask,'' from *The Complete Poems of Paul Laurence Dunbar.* Reprinted by permission of Dodd, Mead & Company, Inc.

P. 66. ''Karma,'' by Edward Arlington Robinson. Copyright © 1925 by Edward Arlington Robinson, renewed 1953 by Ruth Nivison and Barbara R. Holt. Reprinted by permission of The Macmillan Company.

P. 67. ''The Phoenix,'' from *The Cats Cradle-Book,* by Sylvia Townsend Warner. Copyright 1940, Copyright © renewed 1968 by Sylvia Townsend Warner. Reprinted by permission of The Viking Press, Inc.

P. 69. ''Sales-Promotional Genius Available!!!,'' reprinted by permission of C. L. Black.

P. 70. From *I Lost It at the Movies* by Pauline Kael. Copyright © 1964 by Pauline Kael. Reprinted by permission of Little, Brown and Co. in association with the Atlantic Monthly Press.

P. 71. From *The Celluloid Weapon* by David Manning White and Richard Averson. Copyright © 1972 by David Manning White and Richard Averson. Reprinted by permission of Beacon Press.

P. 72. From Hortense Powdermaker's *Hollywood, The Dream Factory,* Little, Brown and Company, Boston, 1950.

P. 73. From Ralph and Natasha Friar's *The Only Good Indian: The Hollywood Gospel,* Drama Book Specialists, New York.

P. 76. ''I Like to Think of Harriet Tubman,'' by Susan Griffin. Copyright © 1972 by Susan Griffin. Reprinted by permission.

P. 78. The Welcome Table,'' Copyright © 1970 by Alice Walker. Reprinted from her volume *In Love & Trouble* by permission of Harcourt Brace Jovanovich, Inc.

P. 82. ''I am Joachín.'' Copyright © 1967 by Rodolfo Gonzales. Reprinted by permission of Rodolfo ''Corky'' Gonzales.

P. 84. From G. C. Payetter's ''How to Get and Hold a Woman,'' in *Up Against the Wall, Mother . . . ,* edited by Elsie Adams and Mary Louise Briscoe, Glencoe Press, Beverly Hills, Ca., 1971.

P. 84. From Joseph Peck's *Life with Women and How to Survive It,* Prentice-Hall, Inc., Englewood Cliffs, N.J., 1961.

P. 85. ''Linguistic Sexism'' reprinted by permission of Ellen Morgan.

P. 86. From ''The Media: New Images of Women in Contemporary Society,'' by Judith Miller and Leah Margulies, in *The American Woman: Who Will She Be?,* edited by Mary Louise McBee and Kathryn A. Blake, Glencoe Press, Beverly Hills, Ca., 1974.

P. 87. From "Playboys Doctrine of Male," reprinted with permission from the April 17, 1971 issue of *CHRISTIANITY AND CHRISIS,* Copyright 1971 by Christianity and Chrisis, Inc.

P. 90. "Woman Defined," from *An Intelligent Woman's Guide to Dirty Words,* published by the Loop YWCA in Chicago. Copyright © 1973 by the Feminist English Dictionary. Reprinted by permission of Ruth Todasco.

P. 91. "Councils," Copyright © 1972 by Marge Piercy from the book *To Be of Use* by Marge Piercy. Reprinted by permission of Doubleday & Company, Inc.

P. 92. From Marcia R. Lieberman, "Some Day My Prince Will Come," December 1972 COLLEGE ENGLISH. Copyright © 1972 by National Council of Teachers of English. Reprinted with permission.

PP. 119, 120, 121, and 129. From *Propaganda and The American Revolution 1763—1783* by Phillip Davidson, University of North Carolina Press, Chapel Hill, N.C., 1941. Reprinted by permission of the University of North Carolina Press.

P. 128. From Carl Berger's *Broadsides and Bayonets,* University of Pennsylvania Press, Philadelphia, 1961.

P. 148. Three quotes taken from *The Birth of the Constitution* by Donald Barr Chidsey. Copyright © 1964 by Donald Barr Chidsey. Used by permission of Crown Publishers, Inc.

PP. 159—160. From *Looking Backward* by Edward Bellamy. Reprinted by permission of New American Library.

P. 161. From H. G. Wells' *When the Sleeper Wakes.*

P. 162. From *1984* by George Orwell. Copyright, 1949 by Harcourt Brace Jovanovich, Inc. Reprinted by permission of Brandt & Brandt, Mrs. Sonia Orwell, and Secker & Warburg.

P. 165. From Aldous Huxley's *Brave New World,* Harper & Row Perennial Classics, New York, 1932.

P. 166. From *The Iron Heel* by Jack London, Grayson Publishing Company. Reprinted by permission of Irving Shepherd.

P. 168. From *Farenheit 451* by Ray Bradbury. Copyright © 1950, 1953, 1967 by Ray Bradbury. Reprinted by permission of Harold Matson Company, Inc.

P. 177. "The Future of Propaganda" reprinted by permission of Richard Watson.

P. 181. From pp 131—137 of "The Social Consequences of the Communications Satellites" in *Voices from the Sky* by Arthur C. Clark. Copyright © 1962 by Arthur C. Clark. Reprinted by permission of Harper & Row Publishers, Inc.

P. 187. From *Future Shock* by Alvin Toffler. Copyright © 1970 by Alvin Toffler. Reprinted by permission of Random House, Inc.

Credits for art

Martha P. Hairston:
pp. 5, 6—7, 34, 48, 58, 131.

Barbara Hack:
pp. 10, 13, 19, 28, 95.

Shirley Sidell:
pp. 16, 16—17, 18, 20, 22, 23, 24—25, 26 top left & bottom, 63, 186.

Culver Pictures, Inc.:
pp. 26 right, 27 top, 70, 72, 73.

Marc and Evelyne Beinheim, Woodfin Camp:
p. 27.

The Dynamics of Change, Kaiser Aluminum & Chemical Corporation © 1967: Bob Fraser. Reprinted by permission:
pp. 32, 155, 159, 160—161, 176 left.

Christine Butterfield:
pp. 67, 68—69, 74 top right, top left & bottom left, 75.

Michelle Vignes:
74 bottom right.

Reproduced from the collection of the Library of Congress:
pp. 98, 99, 100, 101, 102, 103, 104, 105, 106, 112, 114 top & bottom, 118, 120 bottom, 121 top, 123, 125, 133, 136.

Metropolitan Museum of Art; Gift of John S. Kennedy, 1897:
p. 110

New York Public Library, Bancroft Collection:
p. 117.

Philadelphia Museum of Art; Given by Mrs. John D. Rockefeller:
p. 130.

Courtesy NASA:
pp. 154, 165, 181, 189, 195.

M. C. Escher, Reprinted by permission of Escher foundation—Haags Gemeentmuseum—the Hague:
p. 156 *Tetrahedral Planetoide,*
p. 182 *Castle in the Air.*

Kaiser News © 1967. Reprinted by permission:
pp. 164, 168—169, 171, 172, 173, 183—5.

Acknowledgments

We extend special thanks to Dr. Marvin W. Kranz, Specialist in American History of the Library of Congress, for his assistance with materials on the Revolutionary War and the Constitution.

We are also grateful to the following people: Raleigh Wilson, Jr. for agreeing to publish this book; Kenneth Burke for his advice and production expertise; Judith Fillmore for her editorial skills; Christine Butterfield for her imaginative and creative designs which brought so many new dimensions to the book; Pearl Leslie for expert typing and manuscript preparation, and for handling the vitally important but tedious process of obtaining permission to reprint material in this text; Sarah for her encouragement.

Contents

part 1

WHERE ARE WE NOW?   1

    Public Doublespeak   2

A VERBAL MAZE   3

    Defining Propaganda   4

      The Propaganda Machine   5

    Recognizing Propaganda   7

    What Do They Say?   8

      Proper Gander, Teacher   10

      A Fable of Fallacies I   11

      A Matching Game   12

      Doublespeak Doublepuzzle   13

    What Do You Learn in School?   14

PROPAGANDA IN YOUR TOWN   16

    Words That Sell   21

    Uncandid Camera   22

THE SALESMAN IN YOUR HOME   24

    Gestures That Sell   26

    Audio Assaults   27

    Music Can Manipulate Too   28

NEWS AND TRUTH   29

      Unsupported Opinion   30

    Statistics and Reality   32

      Editorial—Man's Best Friend   34

WHAT'S IN THE MAIL?   36

    Testimonials and Name-Calling   37

ADVERTISING ADVERTISING   38

    Great Men Speak of Advertising   38

      An Agency with a Clear Position   39

    Functions of Advertising   40

    Two Views of the Consumer   41

    Politics and Advertising   43

BUREAUCRACY AND VERBAL POLLUTION   46

    Gobbledygook   48

    Watergate Lingo   49

      Wordfact   54

    Doubletalk   58

      Man Bites PG&E   59

      Sales-Promotional Genius Available!!!   60

      Home Buyer's Guide   61

PROPAGANDA IN ART   62

      The Passionate Shepherd to His Love   63

      The Nymph's Reply to the Shepherd   63

Canticle	64
Poem	65
We Wear the Mask	65
Psalm 150	65
The World Is Too Much with Us	66
Karma	66
The Phoenix Sends a Message	67
The Phoenix	67
Persuaders with a Celluloid Weapon	70
Hollywood Perpetuates Myth	72
MINORITY OPINION	75
I Like to Think of Harriet Tubman	76
The Welcome Table	78
I Am Joaquín	82
States' Rights vs. Indian Sovereignty	83
Woman Is	84
Linguistic Sexism—A Neo-Feminist Perspective	85
Playboy Fills a Special Need	89
Woman Defined	90
Councils	91
Learning to Be a Princess	92
The Hand That Rocked the Cradle Points the Way	93
What Shaw Saw—80 Years Ago	94
A Fable of Fallacies II	95

part 2

WHERE DID WE COME FROM?	**97**
PROPAGANDA OF THE PAST	98
SELLING A REVOLUTION	103
Publishing with "Utmost Freedom"	104
Prospect of the Future Glory of America	105
The Argumentative Declaration	107
The Declaration of Independence	107
Visual Persuasion for Unity	108
EXPLAINING THE CRISIS	110
Tom Paine, Master Propagandist	112
Stanzas	113
DIFFERING OPINIONS	114
British Authority versus Congress	115
Lexington: One Event, Two Points of View	116
Broadsides and Bullets	118
Tory Propaganda in America	119
Persuasion for Canada	122
The English Argue among Themselves	124
George III Analyzes the Situation	126

LOOKING BACK AT REVOLUTIONARY PROPAGANDA 127

    A Message for Europeans—Selling

    the New Nation 130

    A Prophecy! 132

        Columbia 132

    Revolution: Blessing or Curse? 134

    Rip Van Winkle Wakes Up to a New Country 135

THE CONSTITUTION: A NEW PROPAGANDA BATTLE 136

    Paine's Pen Endorses the New Government 140

SLAVERY, SLAVES, AND PROPAGANDA 142

    Against Slavery 143

        A Memorial 143

    For Slavery 147

    Slavery Debate at the Constitutional

    Convention 148

    38 Years Later 149

MAKING USE OF THE PROPAGANDA OF THE PAST 150

part 3   WHERE ARE WE GOING? 153

LOOKING FORWARD 154

    Yesterday's Writers Peer into the Future 158

        From *Looking Backward* 158

        From *When the Sleeper Wakes* 161

        From *1984* 162

        From *Brave New World* 165

        From *The Iron Heel* 166

        From *Erewhon* 168

    Today's Writers View Tomorrow 169

        From *Fahrenheit 451* 169

        A Feminist Sees the Future 174

FUTURISTIC MEDIA 176

        A Comment on the Future of

        Propaganda 177

    Free News by A.D. 2000 178

        There's Better Things 179

    Satellites and Sales 181

    Psyche-Service and Psych-Corps 187

LOGIC FROM ANOTHER WORLD 188

        Classified Advertisements 188

        An Astrological Appeal 189

        A Propaganda Proposal from

        Outer Space 190

PROJECTS AND PROJECTIONS 192

        Persuasion Puzzle 193

OVER AND OUT 195

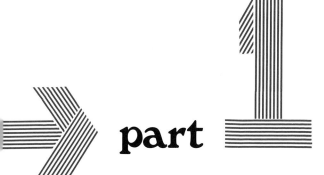

part 1 Where are we now?

National Council of Teachers of English Committee on

Public Doublespeak

BACKGROUND INFORMATION:

Founded in 1911, the National Council of Teachers of English, with headquarters in Urbana, Illinois, is the world's largest subject matter association. Its more than 100,000 members and subscribers support seven major professional journals and more than two dozen new books each year on English and language arts instruction from Kindergarten through graduate school. About 5,000 members attend the annual convention each year, and at that time the Council issues position statements on both professional and public issues. These statements are usually given form in Resolutions passed at the Annual Business Meeting.

Resolutions Passed by the National Council of Teachers of English at the Sixty-First Annual Meeting, 1971:

On Dishonest and Inhumane Uses of Language

Resolved, That the National Council of Teachers of English find means to study dishonest and inhumane uses of language and literature by advertisers, to bring offenses to public attention, and to propose classroom techniques for preparing children to cope with commercial propaganda.

On the Relation of Language to Public Policy

Resolved, That the National Council of Teachers of English find means to study the relation of language to public policy, to keep track of, publicize, and combat semantic distortion by public officials, candidates for office, political commentators, and all those who transmit through the mass media.

In 1972, the NCTE authorized a Committee on Public Doublespeak to implement these resolutions.

Chairman, Daniel J. Dieterich, 807 West Clark Street, Champaign, Ill., 61820

A VERBAL MAZE

propaganda starts here

Your journey through the maze of language used in propaganda

Many influential individuals and groups in American life are misusing language to such an extent that citizens have only the deepest cynicism for the statements made by politicians, government agencies, advertising firms, and other propagandists who bombard them with illogical arguments, emotional appeals, false claims, testimonials, lying statistics, gobbledygook, exaggeration, jargon, and even downright lies.

This book is designed to help you understand the nature of the "propaganda machine" and its influence upon your mind, body, and way of life. The propaganda machine penetrates every aspect of American society. No one is immune to its influence. Much political and commercial propaganda is doublespeak—it says one thing and really means something else. You need to be aware of its influence if you are to be able to reject what is false and misleading and select what is true so that you can make wise judgments as a citizen in this society.

Before examining the diagrammatic propaganda machine, glance through the various definitions of propaganda to get a feel of what the term means. Then look at the propaganda machine itself. It suggests some of the relationships between the various media and the language devices used for propaganda purposes. A few of the terms have been left for you to explore on your own, but most are explained on the following pages.

Defining propaganda . . .

propaganda (prǫpăgae·dă). [a. It. (Sp., Pg.) *propaganda* (F. *propagande*), from the mod L. title *Congregatio de propaganda fide* 'congregation for propagating the faith' : see sense I.]
1. (More fully, *Congregation* or *College of the Propaganda*.) A committee of Cardinals of the Roman Catholic Church having the care and oversight of foreign missions, founded in 1622 by Pope Gregory XV.
    1718 OZELL tr. *Tournefort's Voy. Levant* II. 237 The Congregation of the Propaganda gives them at present but twenty five Roman Crowns a Man. 1819 P. HOPE *Anastasius* (1820) 1. ix. 168 An Italian missionary of the Propaganda. 1851 GALLENGA *Italy* 11. iii. 70 The Propaganda was busy in Paraguay, or Otaheite.
2. Any association, systematic scheme, or concerted movement for the propagation of a particular doctrine or practice.
    Sometimes erroneously treated as a plural (= efforts or schemes of propagation) with singular *propagandum*, app. after *memorandum, -da.*
    1842 BRANDE *Dict. Sci.* etc., sv., Derived from this celebrated society, the name *propaganda* is applied in modern political language as a term of reproach to secret associations for the spread of opinions and principles which are viewed by most governments with horror and aversion. . . . 1879 FARRAR *St. Paul* 1. 208 It seems unlikely that Saul should at once have been able to substitute a propaganda for an inquisition. 1896 *Brit. Weekly* XXII. 340/2 The opportunity and occasion for a vigorous and effective propaganda.
    The Oxford English Dictionary (1933)

prop·a·gan·da (prŏp'əgăn'də), *n.* **1.** the particular doctrines or principles propagated by an organization or concerted movement. **2.** such an organization or concerted movement. **3. College**

prop·a·gan·da (prop'e·gan'de), *n.* [contr. <L. *congregatio de propaganda fide*, the congregation for propagating the faith; see PROPAGATE]. 1. [P-], in the *Roman Catholic Church*, a committee of cardinals, the Congregation for the Propagation of the Faith, in charge of the foreign missions; hence, 2. any organization or movement working for the propagation of particular ideas, doctrines, practices, etc. 3. the ideas, doctrines, practices, etc. spread in this way. 4. any systematic, widespread, deliberate indoctrination or plan for such indoctrination: now often used in a derogatory sense, connoting deception or distortion.
    Webster's New World Dictionary (1968)

prop·a·gan·da (prŏp'ə-găn'də) *n.* **1.** The systematic propagation of a given doctrine or allegations reflecting its views and interests. **2.** Material disseminated by the proselytizers of a doctrine. [From PROPAGANDA.] **—prop'a·gan'·dism'** *n.* **—prop'a·gan'dist** *n.* **—prop'a·gan·dis'tic** *adj.* **—prop'a·gan·dis'ti·cal·ly** *adv.*
Prop·a·gan·da(prŏp'ə-găn'də)**n.** The Congregation of the Roman Curia that has authority in the matter of preaching the gospel and of establishing the Church in non-Christian countries, and of administering Church missions in territories where there is no properly organized hierarchy. [Italian, short for the New Latin title *Sacra Congregatio de Propaganda Fide,* Sacred Congregation for Propagating the Faith, from Latin *prŏpāgñdus,* gerundive of *prŏpāgāre,* to PROPAGATE.]
    The American Heritage Dictionary (1969)

Pro·pa·gan·da \,präp-ə-'gan-də, ,prō-pə-\ *n* [NL. fr *Congregatio de propaganda fide* Congregation for propagating the faith, organization established by Pope Gregory XV] 1 *cap* : a congregation of

prop·a·gan·da (prop'ə·gan'də) *n.* **1.** A systematic effort to persuade a body of people to support or adopt a particular opinion, attitude, or course of action. **2.** Any selection of facts, ideas, or allegations forming the basis of such an effort. **3.** An institution or scheme for propagating a doctrine or system. ■ *Propaganda* is now often used in a disparaging sense, as, of a body of distortions and half-truths calculated to bias one's judgment or opinions. [PROPAGANDA]
Prop·a·gan·da prop'ə·gan'də) *p.* In the Roman Catholic Church, a society of cardinals charged with overseeing the foreign missions, originated by Pope Gregory XV in 1622 as the **Con·gre·ga·ti·o de Prop·a·gan·da Fi·de** (kon·gra·ga'she·o de prop·a·gan'de fi'de) (Congregation for the Propagation of the Faith): with *the.* [< NL (*congregatio de*) *propaganda* (*fide*) (the council for) propagating (the faith) < L, gerundive of *propagare.* See PROPAGATE.]
    Funk & Wagnalls Standard College Dictionary (1963)

propagate, *prop'ə·'gāt, v.t.* to increase by natural process: to multiply: to pass on: to transmit: to spread from one to another: (*obs.*) to increase. **—v.i.** to multiply: to breed. **—adj. prop'agable.** **—ns. propagan'da,** a congregation of the Roman Catholic Church, founded 1622, charged with the spreading of Catholicism (*dē prŏpāgandā fidē,* 'concerning the faith to be propagated'—not a plural but ablative singular): any association, activity, plan, &c., for the spread of opinions and principles, esp. to effect change or reform; **propagand'ism,** practice of propagating tenets or principles: zeal in spreading one's opinions: proselytism; **propagand'ist**—also *adj.—n.* **propaga'tion.—adj. prop'agative.—n. prop'agator.** **—v.t. propage** (prŏ-pāj'; *Congreve*), to beget, prop-

STS PRODUCTION PRESENTS

THE PROPAGANDA MACHINE

Readily available
Powerful
Influential
May be used to run your life

TURN PAGE

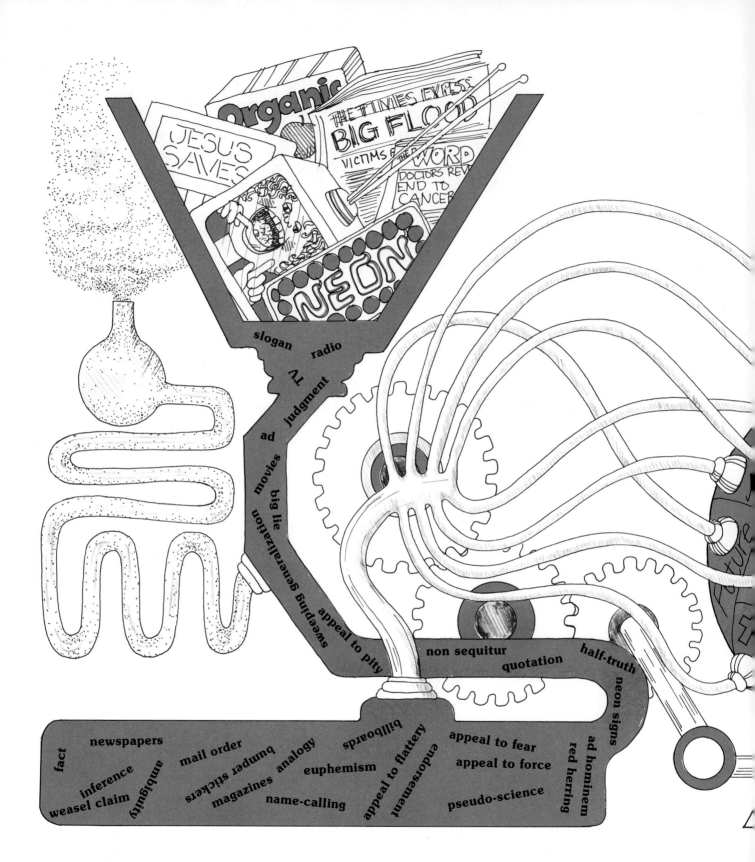

Organic

JESUS SAVES

THE TIMES EXPRESS
BIG FLOOD
VICTIMS F... THE... WORD
DOCTORS REV...
END TO
CANCER

NEON

slogan   radio

TV

judgment

ad

movies

big lie

sweeping generalization

appeal to pity

non sequitur

quotation

half-truth

neon signs

fact   newspapers

inference   ambiguity   mail order

weasel claim   bumper stickers   billboards

magazines   analogy   euphemism   appeal to flattery   appeal to fear

name-calling   endorsement   appeal to force

pseudo-science

ad hominem

red herring

Recognizing propaganda . . .

Propaganda, according to the most cogent authority in the field, is the deliberate attempt to influence mass attitudes on controversial subjects by the use of symbols rather than force. Three factors in this definition deserve special attention: "deliberate attempt," "mass attitudes," "controversial." It is crucial to recognize that it is *intention* that lies at the heart of propaganda. This must be stressed, since it is often crudely assumed that the *effect* of a publication (or a movie) upon those who see or read it determines whether or not propaganda is involved.

Laymen are often confused in the effort to identify propaganda because they find it difficult to distinguish propaganda from education or from patriotic reiterations or from entities of art, barren of ideas. A clear classification at this point will be helpful. Education represents the transmission of aptitudes or attitudes on subjects which are *not* controversial. Patriotic reiterations (pageants, poems, patriotic films) *P* involve the dramatization of accepted political values. Entertainment is the communication of the pleasurable. *N.*

A movie on physiology or golf or *P.* arithmetic is an educational film. A movie which dramatizes the prevailing civic emotions about our country, its institutions or national heroes, is a patriotic film. But a movie made for the *purpose* of changing attitudes about, say, American foreign policy or socialized medicine or monogamy would be a propaganda film.

Leo Rosten

Make a list of situations involving symbols that you think are propagandistic. Then make another list of some that you believe are not propagandistic.

Exchange your lists with another student. Does he or she agree with you?

Discuss any differences of opinion with the whole class.

CLOSEUP: "ERA: THE WAR BETWEEN THE WOMEN"
60 minutes series
INAUGURATION SPECIAL

What do they say?

Speech was given to man to prevent thought.

Bertrand Russell

Most of us are so weary of the constant flood of commercial propaganda that we are inclined to be cynical about anything which affects actions and attitudes. Yet persuasion is not necessarily insincere, dishonest or contrived; and it is sometimes . . . absolutely essential . . . .

Wentworth K. Brown
Sterling P. Olmsted

All propaganda must be popular and its intellectual level must be adjusted to the most limited intelligence among those it is addressed to . . . . All advertising, whether in the field of business or politics, achieves success through the continuity and sustained uniformity of its application.

Adolf Hitler

© 1974, The Register and Tribune Syndicate

Ed Reed

"I write television commercials and I keep getting sick to my stomach."

It is altogether probable that, in spite of their high technical achievements, their constant accessibility, and their relationship to deep human wants and needs, newspapers, radio, movies and advertising are doing as much to arrest as to promote our maturing. In many lives, they appear to weight the scales heavily toward arrested development.

H. A. Overstreet

The average American lives in a media-oriented environment, and try as he may, it is impossible for him to shut these media entirely out of his life.

Robert C. O'Hara

Discuss these excerpts with your classmates.
Choose one and write an exploration of it.

Advertisers have brought the art of propaganda very near to perfection. A consideration of the devices employed in advertisements may help us to recognize the tricks of other propagandists and to understand how immense and insidious is their influence. The advertiser has something to sell; it would be unreasonable to expect him to be disinterested. Accordingly he is unlikely to provide us with all the information that would enable us to form an independent opinion of the value of the article advertised.

L. Susan Stebbing

Meanings are in persons' minds, not in words, and when we say that a word has or possesses such and such meanings, we are really saying that it has evoked or caused those meanings . . . .

Edward L. Thorndike

The fundamental purpose of advertising, the announcing of products, prices, new inventions, and special sales, is not to be quarreled with; such announcements deliver needed information, which we are glad to get. But advertising long ago ceased to restrict itself to the giving of needed information, and its principal purpose, especially in the so-called "national advertising," has become the creating, in as many of us as possible, of automatic reactions. That is to say, there is nothing that would profit the national advertiser more than to have us automatically ask for Coca-Cola . . . .

S. I. Hayakawa

Speech was given to man to disguise his thoughts.

Talleyrand

Proper Gander, Teacher

I was

You were all hatched from eggs.
fact

Each of you will grow to be as big as I am.
inference

Geese are beautiful birds.
judgment

All chickens scare easily.
sweeping generalization

Birds of a feather flock together.
quotation

Visiting dogs can be annoying.
ambiguity

Never follow the advice of ducks. They are a stupid breed of birds.
damning the origin

Tom the turkey is an arrogant show-off.
name-calling

We all know that geese lay golden eggs.
big lie

Geese protect people's property.
half-truth

A Fable of Fallacies I

Read the feature "Proper Gander, Teacher" and the "Fable of Fallacies I." Write out your own example of each of the terms illustrated in the cartoons. Discuss the implications with your classmates.

"Look at Proper Gander," said Bantam Cock. "He struts about with his rubber-hose neck stuck out all the time and thinks he knows everything. I'm glad I don't have to mix with him and those other glamorously plumed avian denizens of the farmyard."

"I love that euphemism," replied the duck. "Just by looking at Gander you can tell all geese are arrogant birds. Anyway, they're different from ducks. That's why I don't like them."

"See the way he waddles when he walks. He's like a drunken bum," sneered the cock. "You can tell how stupid he is."

"Now wait a minute," said Tom Turkey. "You are all making sweeping generalizations, using ad hominem arguments, analogy, and name-calling."

"Who asked for your opinion?" snapped the cock. "You turkeys don't know what you are talking about because you are only good for people to eat at Thanksgiving and at Christmas."

"That's a non sequitur," replied the turkey, "and you'd better watch what you're saying, or I'll peck you into bits and pieces."

The cock parried these appeals to force and fear by crowing noisily and crying, "Watch out! There's a dog coming!" There was no dog in sight.

The turkey started to rush toward the cock, shouting. "Don't try to avoid the issue with your red herring techniques. I'm going to give you what you deserve!"

"Don't be hasty," pleaded the cock, "you know how much I admire you. I think you are the most beautiful and powerful bird in the farmyard. I wish I could be like you. Turkey is King! Turkey is King! I am such a small and insignificant little creature and one of your humble servants."

"Flattery and silly slogans will get you nowhere," the turkey said, "and don't appeal to my pity." And he chased the cockerel off.

Can you add to the list of verbal devices mentioned in the cartoons and in the fable?

fact: I was born in January

All oak trees have acorns.

All Movie stars are famous.

all birds fly south in the fall.

A Matching Game

Here is a list of four terms describing some of the less admirable practices employed by advertisers and other propagandists. The groups of examples illustrate each term. Match the two by putting the number of the word in the blank beside the group that illustrates it.

1. **Pseudo-science**
2. **Flattery**
3. **Weasel words**
4. **Endorsement**

3
Gives *more* miles per gallon.
The *better* face powder.
Helps eliminate odor problems.
Twice as effective as *most* remedies.
The *zingy* refresher.

2
Because you're a special sort of person.
Your ideas created this new toaster.
You won't be fooled by imitations.
You understand why baby's room must be kept spotless.

4
The new champ prefers Martin's.
"In my latest movie, I insisted on wearing Lothario shirts."
"Mon cher, you are sooo intriguing in your Ultra-tech sunglasses."
Twice as many doctors recommend this cough syrup.

1
Only our soap contains LZ-47.
Made with hypo-allergenic ingredients.
Enriched with 44% more body builders.
Scientifically tested for triple strength.

The doublespeak doublepuzzle contains some of the words in the preceding list (the matching game) as well as some media names that appear in the propaganda machine and some that occur in the Proper Gander cartoons and the Fable of Fallacies.

To complete the crossword puzzle, supply the words that fit the following definitions. The initial letter of the correct word already appears in the appropriate box in the puzzle.

ACROSS

1. Insincere praise, deceitful compliments, blarney
7. Message transmission service
8. Ad hominen argument (with 4 down)
10. Catchword; striking phrase associated with particular group, idea, or product
13. Mixture of fact and falsehood (with 27 across)
14. Double meaning
17. To approve—especially a VIP
18. Advertisements (abbreviation)
20. Inoffensive, evasive term for harsher reality
23. To repeat a passage in substantiation or illustration of a point
24. Appears, pretends
26. A diversion intended to distract attention from the real issue (with 30 across)
27. See 13 across
28. Mother _____
29. Coercion, exertion of power
30. See 26 across
31. Arguing against the person rather than against the issue; name-calling (2 words)

DOWN

1. Real things
2. Resemblance, similarity, correspondence
3. Animated images; boob tube
4. Ad hominem argument (with 8 across)
5. Sound receiver
6. Periodical publications
9. Super prevarication (2 words)
11. Inference that does not follow the premise (2 words)
12. "Slippery" word, equivocal, with no real substance (2 words)
15. Celluloid entertainment
16. Honest, dependable, reliable
19. A standard of excellence
21. Deceptive resemblance, not real
22. Conclusion drawn from evidence
25. Knowledge
29. Alarm, apprehension, dismay

What do you learn in school?

One conception of the university, suggested by a classical Christian formulation, is that it be in the world but not of the world. The conception of Clark Kerr, by contrast, is that the university is part and parcel of this particular stage in the history of American society; it stands to serve the need of American industry; it is a factory that turns out a certain product needed by industry or government. Because speech does often have consequences which might alter this perversion of higher education, the university must put itself in a position of censorship.... The University is well structured, well tooled, to turn out people with all the sharp edges worn off, the well-rounded person.

Mario Savio

... Can the college help us use our heads? To think about the function of the college, we have to think about the university as a place which spawns new ideas or breaks through to new visions. A place where we can learn how to use our neurological equipment.

The university, and, for that matter, every aspect of the educational system, is paid for by an adult society to train young people to keep the same game going. To be sure that you do not use your heads. Students, this institution and all educational institutions are set up to anesthetize you, to put you to sleep. To make sure that you will leave here and walk out into the bigger game and take your place in the line. A robot like your parents, an obedient, efficient, well-adapted social game player. A replaceable part in the machine....

Timothy Leary

... The function of higher education, then, is to turn out those industrial cadres, rocket engineers, researchers, planners, personnel managers and development experts needed by the economy. But not only this: our colleges and universities have also been charged with the task of shaping the more ordinary functionaries: the kind who were once not subject to a four-year grind through the educational mill. Looked at in terms of real industrial need these four years of classes, laboratories, football games, hours in the library and bull

WHAT I LEARNED IN SCHOOL THIS YEAR.

I LEARNED HIGH SCHOOL IS CALLED SECONDARY EDUCATION BECAUSE IT TAKES PLACE IN THE SECOND WORLD.

I LEARNED ONLY TO VOLUNTEER WHEN WHAT I HAVE TO SAY AGREES WITH WHAT THE TEACHER HAS TO SAY.

I LEARNED NOT TO BE CURIOUS ABOUT ANYTHING THAT ISN'T ASSIGNED OR THEY CALL YOU A TROUBLE MAKER.

I LEARNED IF YOU HAVE A GOOD TEACHER KEEP IT TO YOURSELF OR THEY GET RID OF HER.

I LEARNED THAT PARENTS HATE TEACHERS ALMOST AS MUCH AS TEACHERS HATE PARENTS BUT NOT AS MUCH AS BOTH HATE KIDS.

I LEARNED INTEGRATION IS WHEN BLACK KIDS SIT TOGETHER IN ONE PART OF THE CAFETERIA AND WHITE KIDS SIT TOGETHER IN ANOTHER.

I LEARNED BUSING IS WRONG —

BECAUSE IT WILL LOWER THE QUALITY OF MY EDUCATION.

©1974 JULES FEIFFER — Courtesy Publishers Hall Syndicate

CAMPUS CLATTER with BIMO BURNS

by Larry Lewis

sessions seem entirely superfluous. But that is not the point. For beyond immediate mechanical requirements there are the larger social imperatives. Social order must be maintained, and the whole fabric of traditions which gives a society its continuity must be kept intact. If this proves to be impossible, then at least appearances must be kept up; patches covering up the rents must be made invisible. As ordinary mechanical tasks multiply, as more of the labor force takes on white-collar jobs and finds itself pushed into the middle class, the process of acculturation becomes increasingly difficult. Formerly, those few who climbed the social ladder learned their manners—were educated to the proper social style—by their gradual exposure to the more or less culturally advanced. This was a slow and haphazard process; many fell by the wayside and never attained the style of life appropriate to their economic station. If the production of consumer goods is to expand, the goods must be consumed. To accomplish this, the new industrial cadres must be prepared for an "enriched"—that is, a cultured—style of life. Above all, the new class must never be allowed to feel that it constitutes a new industrial proletariat. . . .

Louis Kampf

Here are writers who view contemporary education as propaganda for the Establishment. Does your experience confirm or refute their opinion? Write a few paragraphs exploring your reasons for your beliefs.

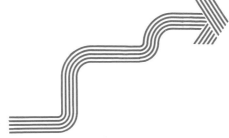

You are the first 21-year-old to be elected Superintendent of Public Instruction. Write the speech in which you explain to the citizenry the purpose of education, and announce the ways in which you will organize educational institutions in order to achieve that purpose.

PROPAGANDA

propaganda in your town

Stand at a busy intersection in your community.
Look all about you, but do not walk more than three steps in any direction.
List all the propaganda appeals you hear and see in ten minutes.

Stand at the busiest spot on your campus, and do the same.

IN YOUR TOWN

What positive appeals are made by the appearance of this supermarket aisle? What negative appeals?

_____
_____
_____
_____
_____
_____
_____

Would it make any difference if you could read any of the signs and labels on the shelves? Explain.

_____
_____
_____
_____
_____
_____
_____
_____
_____
_____
_____

Store window pitches—who are they aimed at?

Locate a billboard with a short slogan as a message. Copy the message in the space below. Beneath that, write a short paragraph stating what background information you need to have in order to understand the message. Next, discuss the appeals being made in the slogan. Do they give you a good opinion of yourself? Why or why not? How?

ENJOY the Sun with us!!

Identify the two contradictory "statements" made in this everyday scene.
What is their significance? What do they say about our society?
If you were a customer who saw this scene upon entering the store, how would you respond?

Words that sell . . .

Clip out a magazine or newspaper advertisement with approximately 100 words of text that urges you to buy a single item. Underline in red the words that explain *what* the ad wants you to buy. Underline in blue the words that tell you *why* you should buy it. Is there a logical connection between them? Explain. What function do the other words serve?

Clip out a magazine or newspaper advertisement with approximately 100 words of text that urges you to take action or accept a specific point of view. Underline in red the words that explain what the ad wants you to do. Underline in blue the words that state why you should take action. Discuss what appeal is being made, and whether you regard that appeal as a reasonable one.

Uncandid camera . . .

Assume that this photograph is part of an advertisement for children's nightgowns. Do you think it would be suitable? What appeal would it make? To whom would it appeal? Discuss in some detail.

Now assume that the same photograph is part of an ad for potted palms. Discuss along the same lines.

Finally, assume that it is part of an ad for luxury homes. Discuss its appeal and suitability.

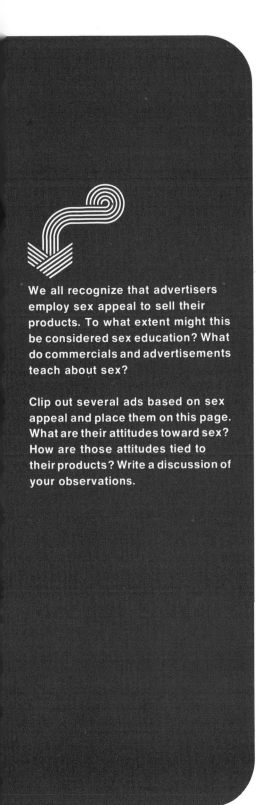

We all recognize that advertisers employ sex appeal to sell their products. To what extent might this be considered sex education? What do commercials and advertisements teach about sex?

Clip out several ads based on sex appeal and place them on this page. What are their attitudes toward sex? How are those attitudes tied to their products? Write a discussion of your observations.

These photographs depicting the same motel are taken from different locations.

Which one would you choose for a Chamber of Commerce brochure about the community in which it is located?

Assume that you had seen one of the photographs and then went to the motel for a night's lodging. Write a letter to your friend describing your reaction to seeing the whole picture.

THE SALESMAN

 What do you think of the TV commercials you currently watch? Select some that you dislike and some that you like, and explore your reasons for disliking or liking each.

Has a TV commercial ever influenced you to buy anything? If so, can you identify what it was about the commercial that hooked you?

Interview people in your community and discover reactions to TV commercials. Which ones were liked or disliked? Why? Compare your findings with those of your classmates.

 Some people believe that a medium such as TV can have an effect even on those who do not watch it. List some ways in which this might occur. Write a few paragraphs discussing the extent to which you believe in the likelihood of such an influence.

Listen to one commercial on TV. What appeal does it make? What other appeals do you hear?

Listen to one TV program. List all the propaganda appeals made in a five-minute segment (excluding commercials).

 Does it sometimes seem that almost the only time anyone smiles on TV is in the commercials? Assume that you are a TV viewer who understands no English. Write out your thoughts as you watch a news broadcast interspersed with numerous commercials.

IN YOUR HOME

"Advertising is 1% innovation and 99% imitation."

"The typical child entering the first grade today has already spent more time watching television than he will devote to the classroom during the next six years. And between one and two of every ten minutes of that television time go to advertising."

Charles Winick

Make a list of TV commercials that use similar techniques to promote different products.

Make a list of TV commercials that are based on similar appeals.

Make a list of TV commercials that employ similar background scenes.

Clip several advertisements and group them according to various similarities.

Mark M. Wards heads a large advertising agency; Susan Shine is his chief copywriter. Using the knowledge you gained from gathering the material for the foregoing exercises, write the conversation the two carry on when they meet to decide on an advertising campaign for a new product.

Watch one hour of commercial children's TV programs. Make a chart showing the basic "lesson" of each segment of the program itself, and the lesson of each commercial. Do these lessons reinforce or contradict one another? Do they reinforce or contradict the lessons the child receives in school? Write a brief analysis.

Now do the same for a very popular adult program.

Gestures that sell . . .

Most Americans are only dimly aware of the impact of nonverbal behavior in the communication process. How aware of it are you?

Watch some TV commercials partly with the sound on and then with the sound off. Focus on the people. Notice the clothes, the facial expressions, the movements of the hands and other parts of the body. What are they telling you?

Does the overall setting—furniture, scenery, buildings—reflect a significant part of the message, too?

Would the verbal message be as effective without its nonverbal accompaniment?

How important is the nonverbal?

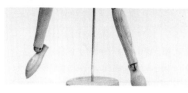

Jot down any nonverbal clichés that you see. The smile will probably be one of them.

Bring your notes to class and share your findings.

Write an essay in which you explore the significance of nonverbal behavior in TV commercials.

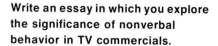

AUDIO ASSAULTS

Listen to a radio program in which the same person speaks both the program material and the commercials. What effect does this presentation have on you as a listener? Does the speaker's tone of voice change for each segment? If so, in what ways? If not, is there any way of knowing when he switches from one segment to another? If someone who did not understand English heard the program, would he realize that two different kinds of messages were being presented? How?

Music can manipulate too . . .

Music has long been used in factories and other places of work to help reduce boredom and heighten productivity among workers engaged in seemingly meaningless, repetitious tasks. It apparently manipulates the feelings of workers so that they are kept alert and therefore more productive, which in turn results in higher profits for the firm concerned.

The same kind of sound manipulation, for a different purpose, is widely used in public places such as restaurants, stores, shopping malls, and dentists' waiting rooms. The effect is intended to be soothing, restful, and entertaining, but it can also have the opposite impact. How often have you sat in a restaurant forced to listen to piped-in music which was too loud and downright displeasing? Music used in this way is impersonal and aimed to please everybody. Unlike radio and TV in your home, you cannot flick a switch and turn it off. You are stuck with it even though your nerves may be crying out for relative quiet so that you can think or talk if you want to.

Stores and other public places that use this so-called "functional" music must believe that the majority of customers welcome or even need it. What do you feel about it? Are you one of those who welcome any kind of music wherever you go?

Visit some public places where "wallpaper" music is used, and some other places that do not use it. Write a passage reflecting your individual appraisal of the two kinds of situations.

NEWS AND TRUTH

THE problem of journalism in America proceeds from a simple but inescapable bind: journalists are rarely, if ever, in a position to establish the truth about an issue for themselves, and they are therefore almost entirely dependent on self-interested "sources" for the version of reality that they report. Walter Lippmann pointed to the root of the problem more than fifty years ago when he made a painful distinction between "news" and truth. "The function of news is to signalize an event, the function of truth is to bring to light the hidden facts, to set them into relation with each other, and make a picture of reality on which men can act." Because news-reporting and truth-seeking have different ultimate purposes, Lippmann postulated that "news" could be expected to coincide with truth in only a few limited areas, such as the scores of baseball games or elections, where the results are definite and measurable. In the more complex and ambiguous recesses of political life, where the outcome is almost always in doubt or dispute, news reports could not be expected to exhaust, or perhaps even indicate, the truth of the matter. This divergence between news and truth stemmed not from the inadequacies of newsmen but from the exigencies of the news business, which limited the time, space, and resources that could be allotted to any single story. Lippmann concluded pessimistically that if the public required a more truthful interpretation of the world they lived in, they would have to depend on institutions other than the press.

. . . Newsmen now almost invariably depict themselves not merely as reporters of the fragments of information that come their way, but as active pursuers of the truth. In the current rhetoric of journalism, "stenographic reporting," where the reporter simply but accurately repeats what he has been told, is a pejorative term used to describe inadequate journalism; "investigative reporting," on the other hand, where the reporter supposedly ferrets out a hidden truth, is an honorific enterprise to which all journalists are supposed to aspire.

Edward Jay Epstein

"Unsupported opinion can be ... a dangerous commodity"

An experienced editor points to some of the reasons for the credibility gap between the media and the public

Opinion in straight news copy, even when labeled clearly, is a dangerous commodity, for it can, even with the best of intentions, as easily distort truth as help clarify it.

Putting aside the ruminations of columnists and commentators (for they stand as declared opinion-givers), opinion is an insidious tool insidiously employed with increasing sophistication. Today's better-informed public is, on the whole, not to be taken in by old crudities (though some writers, broadcasters and editors apparently aren't yet aware). The outrageously biased flat-out statement won't be swallowed. The use of the denigrating photo to accompany a story on a personality of whom the editor disapproves (still a common newspaper, newsmagazine and TV device) is quickly recognized for the news-twisting practice it is.

But what, unfortunately, isn't so readily detected by the casual news reader, radio listener or TV watcher is the calculated use in news copy of weighted words and phrases, the selective use for comment and reaction of individuals favorable to the editor's point of view, the omission of pertinent information needed to understand the information supplied.

In slanted news copy, the "good guy" may be expected, somewhere in the course of the story, to be referred to (unobtrusively but effectively) as "distinguished" or "respected" or in some similar word or phrase, implying reliability; the "bad guy" is "contentious" or something similar, implying reason for doubt. The favored political party may "score a victory" in winning a seat in one part of the country, while the out-of-favor party simply "holds on" in another area. The favored individual, institution or government "states," "declares"; the unfavored "claims." The approved politician "speaks" at a press conference, but his opponent "sweats under the TV lights" (and one who sweats obviously has something to hide).

These are only a few examples. Read carefully, listen carefully, and this too-frequent, subtle and effective shading of the news, calculated to influence its understanding, becomes evident. And behind each weighted report sits an editor who has lost his credentials, either through deceitful intent, sloppy inattention, or blatant dimwittedness.

Omission, too, is highly effective in news-twisting. Again, the editor, the final arbiter, must bear full responsibility. Omitting to provide the context in which a statement has been made can distort the news to a fare-thee-well.

Omitting to background and identify a guest contributor, whose purported job is to report news from his area, not to play the role of opinion-giver, is another device useful in conveying, not the news, but a viewpoint of the news favored by a publication, or a radio or TV station or network. To state simply that the writer is, let us say, a "well-known Washington columnist," tells the reader or listener less than he should know to judge what particular axe (if any) is being ground. And, of course, frequently that is exactly the intent. That "well-known" columnist may, indeed, be notorious among those in Washington for peddling a certain bias. But to those elsewhere in the country where his report is published, without access to that information, his report is presented as straight fact-gathering, untouched by bias or special pleading. Patently, at prime fault, for whatever the reason, is not the guest reporter from Washington, but the editor who has failed to give his readers (or radio or TV audience) information that would put the report in perspective.

My 30 years in news and publishing does not persuade me that such omission in many cases results from editorial carelessness, but from intent. The paper, radio station or TV outlet guilty of that practice has chosen its guest reporter with care, to project a viewpoint that coincides with its own. The editor responsible in such cases has not tampered with the news—he has aborted it.

Unlike proper Victorian children, news editors should not only be not heard, they should be not seen. They should, if they do their job properly, be completely invisible to the audience they serve (while the applause, if any, goes to the writer). But bad editing brings visibility—and hearing, if the editor uses the copy he is responsible for to project his biases.

The difficulties in achieving the goal do not lessen the necessity of it. And it must be an achieved goal, or those within the media who are well along in digging a credibility gap between the media and the public are going to widen gap to gulf that no bridge-building will span.

And if it should be observed that to argue for fact and objectivity in news handling is simply to argue on behalf of "motherhood," then one may ask why it is that "motherhood" in the media these days seems to be in such disrepute.

Keith Knowlton

 Has Knowlton's essay brought you some fresh insights?

Do you agree or disagree with him?
Write an essay in which you support your point of view with examples based on your own observations.

Statistics and reality . . .

My emotions, I found, were being shaped by statistics. Numbers were doing it to me. At the beginning of each month would come the unemployment figures—up to 5.8 percent, down to 5.4 percent, up to 6.0 percent, all seasonably adjusted to affect my mood, like air-conditioning. A week later would come the price-index figures—these were always worse, and my mood went up or down depending on whether things were getting worse faster or slower. Prices were up 0.7 percent in a bad month, up 0.4 in a good month. Then would come crime figures; and housing figures; and export-import figures; trade-balance figures; school figures; divorce figures; finally Gross National Product figures, and these always baffled me. What were they? What did they measure? In whose web was I caught?

Theodore H. White

Emphasis, omission, *and* distortion *rather than out-right lying are the tools of the war propagandists.*

Of all the weird statistics emanating from MacArthur Headquarters none was stranger than its estimate of November 4 as to the size of the North Korean forces. Six days earlier, on October 30, "a spokesman for General MacArthur" said in Tokyo that the North Korean Army had suffered 460,000 casualties in dead, wounded, and captured, and had only 37,000 men left, including guerrillas. On November 4, a spokesman at MacArthur Head-quarters said the North Koreans "now had at least elements of twelve divisions and five independent brigades in the northern area." The New York Times correspondent noted that at the peak of North Korea's war effort it had only thirteen divisions in the field, and added that the enemy "apparently had an almost equal number of organizations again available for action, although some of the present 'divisions' probably numbered only a few thousand men."

I. F. Stone

Statistics, for us, fall naturally into various colors. For instance, 7,377,777, whether it stands for imports or exports, is undoubtedly red. But 1,019,901 is a pale, light, cool, grayish blue. And can anyone doubt that 525,555,555,555 is of a bright aggressive yellow color, and gives off a high pitched note from the rapid motion of its myriad pinions? There is something querulous and peevish and impatient about 525,555,555,555, too; we shall not admit it into the volume of statistics which we are compiling.

Hitherto there has been a science of statistics, but no art. That is, no avowed art. We suspect that certain advanced statisticians really approach the subject as we do, joyfully and all unshackled. But they pretend to be staid and dry and sober. They have respectable positions in the community to maintain. After compiling several pages of statistics full of sound and color, just for the sheer glee of reveling in sensation, they become cowards and conceal their glee; they write industrial and financial and sociological articles around their lovely tables and twist them into proving something important. They conceal their art, they muffle and smother their finer impulses beneath a repellent cloak of science. They are afraid that their toys will be taken away from them if they play with them frankly, so they affect some sort of useful employment.

We remember reading somewhere, and it was cited as an example of the mental twilight of the Middle Ages, that learned clerks and doctors were accustomed to debate the question as to how many angels could stand on the point of a needle. But these medieval disputants were not stupid at all. They were quite right to be interested in such things. They were wise enough to divorce statistics from reality utterly. Things of every sort—all the arts and philosophies—suffer today because we insist on connecting them with trivial reality. We try to make them prove something. We try to set them to work. And definite proofs will not always be tiresome, and work a thing to be escaped. People are not really enthusiastic about having things proved to them or about working; they want to have a good time. And they are quite right, too.

Statisticians deal with precious, intangible stuff, with the flecks and atomies of faery—and how few of them dare rise to the full possibilities of their medium! They are merely foolish when they might so readily achieve insanity if they had but the courage to be themselves.

There are, for instance, 1,345 statisticians in this land who would know, if they were laid end to end, that 4,988,898,888 is green in color, a deep, dark green. Yet they are all afraid to stand forth like men and say so; they are afraid of what people will think of them. They are obsessed with the belief that materials are significant, without stopping to reflect that, even were this so, significance would still remain immaterial.

Don Marquis

Man's Best Friend

Dogs are said to be "man's best friend," yet dogs in America are fast becoming one of man's most pestilential problems. Reliable statistics, gathered from all over the country, prove that unwanted mutts are increasing by the millions. A spot check of any dog pound or pet shop will reveal the fact that unwanted puppies and dogs of all ages and sexes are brought in by the thousands to be disposed of (often in a barbarous and cruel manner).

The reason is that owners of mongrels are irresponsible and traitorous where their pets are concerned. A family will buy a cute puppy from a pet shop and bring it home where it becomes "part of the family." But as soon as that dog grows up into its ugly maturity, it becomes unwanted and uncared for. It is left to roam the neighborhood, catch diseases, and breed with any other dog it can come into contact with. Many dogs have been known to travel miles in search of sex. Some are run over by cars and left to die.

There are other aspects of the problem, too. In my neighborhood, which is representative of millions of others in the nation, it is impossible to walk a block away from my house without being snarled and barked at. The mailman and the newspaper boy can substantiate that. One is lucky not to be severely bitten. My lawn is used by the neighbors' dogs as a daily depository. The stench on a hot summer's day is unimaginable. And things do not end there. It is impossible to get to sleep after a hard day's work because itinerant dogs bark at the moon all night or at something else. To my knowledge, no ecology group has fought to silence dogs, a major cause of noise pollution in any residential area.

There are too many dogs, and their numbers are increasing at mind-boggling rates. Something must be done about it.

I have a solution. Let's eat them.

Many cultures in the world consider dogs a great delicacy. GI's stationed in the Philippines have found dog meat delicious. If Americans could adjust their eating habits a little, then the present meat shortage and high cost of meat could be safely ignored. Any doctor will tell you that dog meat is chock-full of protein.

Animal pounds and pet shops should be licensed to sell dressed dog meat at bargain prices. This would be much more practical and less wasteful than the present method of killing and disposing of dogs, or sending large quantities of unfortunate canines to be experimented upon in laboratories. Any dog lover hates that situation.

Several plump puppies, roasted, would make a fine meal for a large family. Older dogs, which tend to get a bit stringy, could be used in stews or casseroles. I am convinced that the imaginative and creative American housewife could think up dozens of tasty menus made from dog meat. And what a saving to the family budget!

My solution has the additional advantage of turning a traitorous and irresponsible citizenry into patriotic providers of cheap and succulent food for the nation. And that's a real consideration in these days of inflation.

Examine this editorial for for evidence of loaded words and other propaganda devices such as unsupported opinions, appeal to pity, bandwagon approach, half-truths, cultured bias, oversimplification, name-calling, abused statistics, sampling, wit, and humor. Share your findings with your classmates.

Clip some current editorials from local or national newspapers and mark loaded words and other persuasive devices. Does this kind of close analysis help you to understand more clearly what is really being said?

Do the writers of these letters appear to have read the editorial carefully?

One writer says the editorial is "packed with . . . fallacies." Do you agree? How many can you detect in the editorial and in the letters?

Letters to the editor

Dear Sir:
Yesterday morning, I read your editorial to my husband, and we knew you were kidding. But our dachsie took you seriously. He gave me the dirtiest of looks, tucked his tail between his legs, and hurried to his basket. There he covered himself with blankets, and hasn't peeped out since.

Frannie Smith
Bend, Ore.

Sir:
Thank goodness someone has come up with a good idea about the dog situation in this country. It's not the dogs, but the dog-freaks, who are the menace, though.

Sue Imhof
Michigan Falls, Iowa

Sir:
The editorial on dogs is packed with sloppy logic, misuse of statistics and fallacies. I don't even think it's funny. It's just a lot of dog-wash.

Barbara Vanwyck
Little Falls, Mo.

Sir:
With food prices as high as they are today, I think the idea of eating dogs is fantastic. I am going to the dog pound to buy myself some cheap meat. Why hasn't someone thought of this before?

Derek Montavi
Bronx, NYC

Sir:
Your editorial recommending eating dogs was positively disgusting. The worst thing about it was calling that revolting idea "patriotic." It is obvious that the whole thing was dreamed up by some foreigner trying to destroy American ideals. You can always spot these creeps. We ought to send guys like that back where they came from!

Bruce Schoenfeld
Hyattsville, Md.

Sir:
The writer of this editorial must be putting me on. It's just a take-off on Jonathan Swift's Modest Proposal. Hah!

Mike Hansen
U. of C., Santa Cruz, Calif.

Dear Sir:
In our English class at Merlin High, we discussed your editorial about dogs. The captain of the track team supported it—he said you're really with it. And two of our best cheer leaders said it was a right-on job. The class voted, and the majority was on your side.

We just thought you'd like to know there's no generation gap when it comes to dogs.

Jeb Washington
Montague, Ala.

Madam:
If they eat dogs in the Philippines, then they must be lousy people living over there. I was planning a trip to Manila, but, after reading the editorial, I canceled it.

Pogo Binker
Exeter, Conn.

Madam:
Why fuss over a bit of mess in our streets or on our lawns? Dogs behave in the way Nature made them, and surely we should not go against Nature.

Jody McKeough
Chicago, Ill.

WHAT'S IN THE

BY ACTING IMMEDIATELY YOU CAN APPLY FOR THIS VALUABLE
TERM LIFE INSURANCE POLICY
that Can Give Your Family An Additional
$10,000.00
BUT HURRY! THIS OPPORTUNITY IS TIME-LIMITED. YOU MUST REPLY
BEFORE MIDNIGHT OF THE DATE SHOWN ABOVE!

Today--everywhere, living costs are soaring sky high. So
much so, that your present life insurance probably falls far short
of providing your family sound financial security.

If something should happen to you, wouldn't you want your
family to have enough money standing by--without having to turn to
friends or relatives for help?

The prestige and authority of the
Academy are such that scholars and
statesmen of all political persuasions
have enrolled as members. To retain its representative character, the
Academy extends invitations of membership to concerned people with
widely varying interests and political
convictions.

If you often wish you could feel less pressured, more in touch with
the natural world...if you're sometimes nettled by how much other
people (perhaps even your own children) seem to know about science
...then Museum membership is well worth your consideration.

Barricaded from nature by concrete and brick, forbidden by glass
from touching, prohibited by asphalt from pausing, too many of us
nowadays risk becoming the intellectual shut-ins that Thomas Huxle
once described:

> "To a person uninstructed in natural history, his country or
> seaside stroll is a walk through a gallery filled with wonderful
> works of art, nine-tenths of which have their faces turned to
> the wall."

What NATURAL HISTORY (magazine) does each month is turn those
hidden works around so you can share your knowledge with your chil
dren, and apply it to your family adventures with nature: afternoon
walks, days at the shore, weekends in the country, vacations.

mail?

The most common propaganda consists of the letters we receive every day—for fund raising, magazine-subscription renewals, election materials, support for causes. Here are some samples. Which techniques do you note in each?

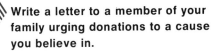 Write a letter to a member of your family urging donations to a cause you believe in.

Now write a letter addressed "Dear Occupant" urging donations to your cause.

Why were changes necessary? Did they improve your letter or impair it? In what ways?

Graduates of UNCF schools live and work in communities all across the country. They can be found in the hallowed halls of Harvard, and on the backroads of America's rural towns; sitting on the highest court in the land, or at the bedside of a sick and forgotten old man. In every walk of life they will be found constantly striving to give back the fruits of ed- ucation--education that you can help make a reality.

THE LIBRARY OF URBAN AFFAIRS
is a book club. A most unusual one.
By mass standards, it's small.
By anybody's standards, it's select.
In reputation and influence, it's enormous.

Testimonials and name-calling . . .

Read a statement that makes use of either direct or implied testimonials. Make a chart showing the following:

    Speaker

    Testimonial statement

    Author of testimonial

    Reason for its use

 Write a well-developed paragraph in which you discuss the effect the testimonial had on you. Did it persuade you to accept the speaker's position? Discuss the reasons. If it did not, consider why the testimonial did not achieve the desired effect.

 Write a short testimonial on a subject of your own choosing. Exchange your testimonial with another classmate and write about how his testimonial affected you.

Read a political statement that engages in name-calling. Make a chart showing the following:

    Speaker

    Opponent

    Name used for opponent

    Intended effect

 Write a well-developed paragraph in which you discuss the effect the name-calling had on you. Did it make you dislike the speaker's opponent? Consider why. If it did not, explore the reasons why the speaker failed to achieve the effect she desired.

Great men speak of advertising . . .

Advertising nourishes the consuming power of men. It sets up before a man the goal of a better home, better clothing, better food for himself and his family. It spurs individual exertion and greater production.

Sir Winston Churchill

If I were starting life over again, I am inclined to think that I would go into the advertising business in preference to almost any other. . . . The general raising of the standards of modern civilization among all groups of people during the past half century would have been impossible without the spreading of the knowledge of higher standards by means of advertising.

Franklin D. Roosevelt

Advertising, no less than art, is founded on eternal verities.

The latter responds to our aspiration to be something more than human: the former to a perverse insistence on remaining something less, manipulable objects in the service of notions like "success" or "happiness."

Thomas Albright

Every alert person must recognize that advertising has been a stimulating influence in our modern civilization. It often has stimulated people to want the new and desirable. As such, advertising may be considered an "accelerator of civilization." We now have more facilities for comfort than the preceding generations, which had no automobiles, airplanes, or television sets. We believe that such devices contribute to better living. . . .

Advertising helps to bridge the gap between undeveloped resources and informs people of the good things available to them. One reason why advertising has been more potent here than in some other countries is that we have the kind of people who differ from those of other countries: our people assume that anything that is satisfactory today can be made even better tomorrow.

Advertising contributes toward the greater availability of goods. Purchasing power is not a static quantity, like water in a bucket or the number of seats in a theater. Actually, the quantity of goods and services that people can buy in a year depends not only on the quantity of purchasing power but also on the rapidity of turnover, the ''velocity of the dollar.'' Advertising speeds up the turnover of trade, and the result is a greater annual volume of individual purchases. . . .

Effective advertising tends to lower the price of goods to the customer because costs of production and selling are reduced when goods are produced and sold in large quantities. . . .

Harry Walker Hepner

This is the time of transition from the commercial age, when it was the production and distribution of commodities which occupied the ingenuity of men. Today we have moved from the production of packaged goods to the packaging of information. Formerly we invaded foreign markets with goods. Today we invade whole cultures with packaged information, entertainment, and ideas.

Herbert Marshall McLuhan

An Agency with a Clear Position

"Our kind of advertising."

We start with the individual in creating our messages. We use research to help us know and understand, as a person, the prospect for our product—not a set of demographics but as a unique human being with whom we can communicate on a personal basis.

We think of advertising not as a way to tell her what we want her to know about a product, but as a means of showing her how that product fits into her life in a beneficial way.

We let the personality of the advertiser come through more than that of the advertising because we know a dialogue is more productive than a lecture.

We use advertising to build businesses rather than one-time purchases.

Our advertising approaches the individual with a respect for his sense and sensibilities.

It gets into people's hearts, not under their skins.

It makes friends as well as sales.

This kind of human, personal advertising has helped our clients grow. It's helping us grow. But no matter how gratifying their growth or ours, we'll take more pride in being a warm agency than a "hot" one.

John E. O'Toole
President, Foote, Cone & Belding

Functions of advertising . . .

As a Tool of Selling. Advertising is, above all, *a tool of selling*—its primary function is that of a salesman. But in performing that function fully, advertising is also an instrument of education, a molder of public opinion, and a builder of public relations.

As Education. Advertising, as educator, speeds the adoption of the new and untried and, in so doing, accelerates technological advances in industry and hastens the realization of a fuller life for all. It helps reduce accidents and waste of natural resources, and contributes to building a better understanding and appreciation of American ideologies.

As a Molder of Opinion and Goodwill Builder. Advertising, as a molder of opinion, sells goods, but in addition it helps win elections, builds faith in a democratic way of life, and becomes the keystone of a free competitive economy.

As an instrument of public relations, advertising sells goods, but it also assists in maintaining goodwill among the various group interests that must function in harmony in a democracy.

Walter A. Gaw

The author of this statement sees advertising as a positive force in the American capitalist society. He believes it educates people in ways that support ecology and technological advancement, and that it creates enlightened voters who can function in an informed and effective way in a democracy.

But other experts in public affairs believe that advertising helps win elections by "selling" a candidate as though he were a commodity. In such a campaign, more emphasis is placed on the candidate's image than on his reality; his statements are modified to meet the public demand, rather than expressing his true beliefs.

Which attitude do you feel dominates American political life? What evidence supports your belief?

Revise the quotation by Walter A. Gaw so that it states your personal position in a very precise manner.

Two views of the consumer . . .

Since we are achievement-oriented rather than satisfaction-oriented, we always think of ourselves first as producers and only second as consumers. We talk of the "beleaguered consumer" as if this referred to some specialized group of befuddled little old ladies.

To some extent this convention is a maneuver in the American war between the sexes. Since men dominate production and women consumption, the man who produces shoddy merchandise can blame his wife for being incompetent enough to purchase it for him. Men have insulated themselves to this extent from having to deal with the consequences of their behavior.

What all of our complex language about money, markets, and profits tends to mask is the fact that ultimately, when the whole circuitous process has run its course, we are producing for our own consumption. When I exploit and manipulate others, through mass media or marketing techniques, I am also exploiting and manipulating myself. The needs I generate create a treadmill that I myself will walk upon. It is true that if I manufacture shoddy goods, create artificial needs, and sell vegetables, fruit, and meat that look well but are contaminated, I will make money. But what can I do with this money? I can buy shoddy goods and poisoned food, and satisfy ersatz needs. Our refusal to recognize our common economic destiny leads to the myth that if we all overcharge each other we will be better off.

Philip Slater

The consumer is king, in our free enterprise system. His wants, translated into purchases, will determine the extent to which we utilize our productive capacities as well as the standard of living of our people.

Harry Walker Hepner

Do you think of yourself as a consumer? Do you regard purchasing as woman's work? How do these attitudes affect your reactions to advertising?

We are all consumers. Do you feel like a king? Explain why or why not.

Choose one of your favorite possessions, and write a highly enthusiastic advertisement, of approximately 100 words, designed to sell it. Now write a 100-word description of the object which is as factual, objective, balanced, and complete as you can make it. Discuss the differences between the two statements. What information did you omit from the advertisement? Why? What information did you give in the ad which is not in the objective description? Why? Do you believe your description would succeed in selling your possession?

Based on this analysis, write an essay on the ethics of advertising, discussing the obligations of the advertiser to give complete information to the consumer.

Politics and advertising . . .

Politicians and interest groups have long been aware of the success of the skills and techniques used by commercial advertising agencies to move billions of dollars worth of merchandise. And they have rightly felt that the kind of advertising techniques which are designed to help men and women make up their mind as to what to buy could also be successfully used to help voters decide in which direction they should vote.

This is one important reason why it has become patently obvious to the observant newspaper reader and TV viewer that the participation of public-relations men and advertising agencies in partisan politics is extensive. Another reason for the ever-increasing reliance of politicians on the help of public-relations counsel is that political interests are fully aware of the increasing technical complexity of the mass-media machinery.

Twenty-five years ago, TV was a comparative toy

The rapid technological expansion of the mass media has called for new skills and techniques. Twenty-five years ago, TV was a comparative toy. Today it blankets the nation, utilizing techniques and offering persuasion possibilities peculiar to itself. The steady hammering of commercial advertising on TV and radio has served to deaden the receptive faculties of many listeners. A continuing program researching fresh ideas and gimmicks is essential to future advertising success. With a mushrooming population, especially in California, the need for printed matter has doubled and trebled, adding tremendously to the already difficult problems of distribution.

The present magnitude of the public-relations profession owes much of its scope to the growth of the mass media of communication. Professional public-relations men make it a policy to follow and keep abreast of the latest techniques required by an expanding mass media.

During the course of a political campaign, the political public-relations man must compete not only with the opposition, but with the day-to-day news, soap operas, murder mysteries, and other shows designed to entertain the public.

If he is to succeed in getting his fair share of the voter's attention, then the mass-media propagandist must try to present his radio or TV message as close to the popular shows as possible. This way, he cashes in, as it were, on interest already aroused. Even so,

Most every American loves contest

in the limited time at his disposal, he must reach the strong emotions like anger or fear if he is to break through the barrier of apathy that most people display toward political pitches.

> The average American, when you catch him after hours, as we must, doesn't want to be educated; he doesn't want to improve his mind; he doesn't even want to work, consciously, at being a good citizen.
>
> But there are two ways you can interest him in a campaign and only two that we have ever found successful.
>
> Most every American loves *contest*. He likes a good, hot battle, with no punches pulled. He likes the clash of arms! So you can interest him if you put on a fight! . . .
>
> Then, too, most every American likes to be entertained. He likes the movies; he likes fireworks and parades. . . .
>
> So if you can't fight, put on a show! And if you put on a good show, Mr. and Mrs. America will turn out to see it.

This statement made by Clem Whitaker, one of the founders of Whitaker & Baxter, Campaigns, Inc. (a major political public-relations firm), is reported by

Stanley Kelley, Jr., in his book *Professional Public Relations and Political Power*. It reflects the basic tactics used in modern political campaigns on behalf of candidates and other political goals.

Once in the hands of a political public-relations agency, the political candidate is managed much in

Gimmicks may consist of simple jingles such as, "Vote Yes on Four to close that door." The number *four* would represent the number of the initiative on the ballot, in this case advocating passage of a law designed to force people to lock their doors every time they leave their houses.

Vote yes on four to close that door

the same way as an actor is handled by a theatrical agent. The public-relations firm arranges radio and TV spots, reserves speaking engagements, writes speeches, and generally sees to it that the candidate lives up to the character given him by a carefully prepared buildup.

However, if it is an Initiative or Recall being advocated or attacked, attention-arresting novelties or gimmicks are often used. The purpose of these is to attract the attention of people who are too pre-occupied to be much interested in politics.

Sometimes the gimmick is in the form of a picture or drawing. An overfat pig wallowing in a pool of gasoline with the slogan "Ban the gas guzzlers" might be used on billboards during a campaign advocating the abolition of all cars that get less than twelve miles to the gallon.

The possibilities of gimmicks are endless. Sometimes gimmicks may have dramatic appeal, yet really obscure the issues. Their main function, though, is to grab and hold attention and, hopefully, attract a lot of favorable votes in the ballot booth.

Watch for gimmicks that are used in radio and TV commercials, and in magazines and newspaper ads. Catchy tunes and jingles are usually gimmicks to get attention. Have you noticed any others?

Much has been given us, and much will rightfully be expected from us. We have duties to others and duties to ourselves; and we can shirk neither.

Theodore Roosevelt, Inaugural Address
March 4, 1905

Our program is never to oppress, but always to assist. But while we do justice to others, we must require that justice be done to us.

Calvin Coolidge, Inaugural Address
March 4, 1925

These dark days will be worth all they cost us if they teach us that our true destiny is not to be ministered unto, but to minister to ourselves and our fellow men. . . . If I read the temper of our people correctly, we now realize as we have never realized before our interdependence on each other; that we cannot merely take but we must give as well. . . .

Franklin D. Roosevelt, First Inaugural Address
March 4, 1933

And so, my fellow Americans: ask not what your country can do for you—ask what you can do for your country.

My fellow citizens of the world: ask not what America will do for you, but what together we can do for the freedom of man.

John F. Kennedy, Inaugural Address
January 20, 1961

In our own lives, let each of us ask not just what will government do for me, but what can I do for myself?

Richard M. Nixon, Second Inaugural Address
January 20, 1973

BUREAUCRACY

Verbal pollution can take varied forms, including jargon, code words, bureaucratic language, and other types of unintelligibility.

Translate each of these statements into clear English.

Write a few paragraphs speculating on why people write this kind of muddled language. What do they achieve? Why do they want to achieve it?

Because of the unexpected level of inquiries we have had about the materials we are developing for use in the classroom, we have been forced to readjust our plans regarding the printing of the educational packages.

_____

_____

_____

_____

_____

_____

_____

Amounts shown in the eligible for major medical column have been applied to the deductible required by your contract.

_____

_____

_____

_____

Personnel procedural policies were finalized by the Ad Hoc Committee of the Management Classification Administration Council and their implementation now becomes the sole responsibility of the Supervisorial Board.

_____

_____

_____

_____

_____

_____

_____

AND VERBA

Applicants otherwise eligible who seek to transfer from other institutions of collegiate rank but whose college records fail to show a satisfactory scholarship average may be admitted only when the deficiency has been removed by additional work completed with grades sufficiently high to offset the shortage of grade points.

_____

_____

_____

_____

_____

_____

_____

_____

_____

Applications must be filed not later than two (2) calendar months before the initial date of that quarter or session in which graduation will occur. Applications favorably processed will be duly returned to successful applicants through the auspices of the Student-Faculty Executive Committee.

_____

_____

_____

_____

_____

_____

_____

_____

_____

_____

_____

GOBBLEDYGOOK

agreement in principle *(cliché)*, meaning, "We'll never solve this one but it's not worth fighting about."

an important announcement *(advertising phrase)*, euphemism for a sales talk read into forty million deserted living rooms while folks out in Televisionland put fresh heads on beer.

bipartisanship, *n.,* a political truce during which each party rifles the other's files for ammunition in the next campaign.

classified, *adj. (bureaucratese),* epitaph for a high-level blunder.

conformist, *n.,* anyone who does not take exception to the same things you do.

definitize, *v. (Pentagonese),* signifying the act of exhuming a "finalized" decision when Congress demands an autopsy.

finalize, *v. (bureaucratese),* signifying formal adoption of a decision, policy or program, with tacit agreement that it be given a quiet burial, or "implemented."

freudian, *adj.,* description for a philosophy which enables you to blame your parents for whatever goes wrong.

The National Society for the Preservation of the English Language to Say What You Mean has issued solemn warnings from its annual conclave here against the accelerating debasement of the mother tongue. All purists have been cautioned to exercise particular care in approaching terminology injected into the language by the ad man, the bureaucrat and the psychiatrist—"those masters of the fluent cliché, the deceptive euphemism, the meaningless polysyllabic, and pompous argot," to quote the society's interim report.

As a guide for its members, the society has also compiled the following dictionary of "dangerously corruptive" words and terms with accompanying translations or definitions in pure English.

---

great, *adj.* (a) theatrical; applied to a performance that will be remembered until second drink of after-theatre party; (b) sports; any contest played before television cameras; (c) political; any candidate not in prison at campaign time.

implement, *v. (bureaucratese),* what you do to carry out a decision, policy, or program when you are doing nothing.

individualist, *n.,* what you are.

know-how, *n.,* singular mental capacity peculiar to persons of United States residence (therefore commonly called "American know-how") which guarantees that Russia cannot put up an earth satellite until spies filch American secret of how to do it.

liberal, *n.,* anyone whose ideas coincide with yours.

middle-of-the-roader, *n.,* a politician convinced it will cost him votes to be caught with an idea.

summit meeting, *n.,* a convention of top brass for press and propaganda group-portrait sittings.

team, *n.,* a mutual protection society formed to guarantee that no one person can be held to blame for a botched committee job that one man could have performed satisfactorily.

top priority *(cliché),* a precise translation would be: "This may be idiotic, but it's the boss's idea."

Russell Baker

Study this essay carefully by making note of the major points raised in each section. Then draw the items on your list together and write a summary, in your own words, of what Gambino has said.

Watergate Lingo: *A Language of Non-Responsibility*

by Richard Gambino

We operated on what is known in some industries as a zero-defect system. We attempted to get everything right.

H. R. Haldeman

In a now famous phrase, Ron Ziegler and John Ehrlichman have declared White House statements proven false to be "no longer operative." This is a very handy phrase which can mean any of the following:

It wasn't true in the first place.

I'm sorry I said it.

I thought it was true then but I know now it wasn't.

While the public was left wondering what the phrase meant, responsibility for the original lies was shifted from the liars to the lies themselves. The responsibility was not in the people, not even in the stars, but in the statements themselves, which were spoken of as if they had lives and energy of their own.

In ordinary English we speak of employees being fired. In the language of the Department of State, they are "selected out." It sounds as if the fired people are honored. The palliative phrase relieves the employer from responsibility for an unpleasant act. Similarly, at the C.I.A., according to Director Colby, superiors do not fire subordinates. They "arrange a circumstance where employees can be helped to leave government service early." How helpful of them! One is almost led to think that people dismissed might thank their bosses for being favored.

Those involved in Watergate or its cover-up do not destroy evidence of crimes. They "deep-six" papers. This sailor's phrase conjures up colorful salts jettisoning unneeded ballast over the side instead of political men engaged in criminal conspiracy. The frequent use of metaphors and similes to sugar-coat questions of culpability reached a high point when Special White House Counsel J. Fred Buzhardt waxed poetic about his predecessor, John W. Dean III. Instead of saying that Dean's testimony was false, Buzhardt spoke of "the failure of Dean's muse while he was on the mountain. . . . " Now if Dean were lying under oath he would be guilty of perjury and could be held legally accountable. But it seems cruel and unusual punishment to declare one a liar and perjuror merely because his muse failed while he was on the mountain. After all, who among us has not known frustration in our creative enterprises?

Whether Dean's muse was reliable or not, he said during his testimony that those engaged in the cover-up once suggested that John Mitchell "should be brought forward." Connotations of going to the head of the class leap to mind. The phrase also evokes one coming forward with forthrightness, sincerity and even courage. Through the magic of words, those who made the suggestion that

Mitchell take all the guilt and punishment for all the conspirators sound like honest brokers, even like outraged righteous souls. As long as their language is used, it becomes impossible to blame them for wanting to make one man the patsy for a conspiracy to obstruct justice.

When Mitchell finally did come forward (in the ordinary sense of the term), he spoke to the Senate Select Committee about "White House horror stories." Not criminal conduct or unethical behavior by White House officials and employees, but "White House horrors." "Criminal conduct" and "unethical behavior" are depressingly meaningful expressions. They lead to thoughts of real acts by real people with real names and faces who really can be and should be held responsible. But "White House horror stories" suggests vague, perhaps unreal, events caused by nameless occult or imaginary powers. The phrase places the Watergate crimes and other misconduct in the same categories as silly old wives' tales of haunted houses and Hollywood fantasy. Although we are frightened by these horror stories, we know our fears are baseless. It is only gentle, benign Boris Karloff behind the terrible Frankenstein mask. Don't be scared kiddies.

If Hugh Sloan, Jr. gave money to a convicted criminal one might suspect him of something rotten. But if as it was said he merely paid "increments . . . in the form of currency" to G. Gordon Liddy, why Sloan sounds as if he was merely giving his fellowman his due. After all, increments are normally thought to be deserved. And "currency" is what scholarly economists deal with, a far cry from the filthy lucre you and I covet. Could Sloan be guilty of something illegal or immoral? Why it is unthinkable—because Washingtonspeak makes it literally unspeakable.

The decline of language

Because of the language they use, and in which we are compelled to follow their accounts, Watergate witnesses and the people they favor are never really responsible. Even those seeking the truth are forced into parlance in which moral and legal responsibility is unutterable. Thus Senator Howard Baker, vice-chairman of the Senate Select Committee, asked one of the witnesses, "how we might ventilate the structure of campaigning." One who ventilates a structure—presumably one who causes air to flow through a building—is not per se doing anything or concerned with anything of any moral or legal consequence whatsoever. His behavior is morally and legally neither responsible or irresponsible. It is quite different with a person who attempts to reform illegal and unethical political campaigning, a sticky matter for many on both sides of the Senate hearing table. Better to talk about ventilation.

Many commentators on the Watergate actions have ominously linked the events with the society presented in George Orwell's novel *1984*. As I have watched the Watergate hearings on television, I have been reminded not so much of *1984* as of a lesser known work of Orwell, an essay written in 1945 entitled, *Politics and the English Language*. In it, Orwell warned:

> It is clear that the decline of a language must ultimately have political and economic causes . . . But an effect can become a cause, reinforcing the original cause and producing the same effect in an intensified form, and so on indefinitely. A man may take to drink because he feels himself to be a failure, and then fail all the more completely because he drinks. It is rather the same thing that is happening to the English language. It becomes ugly and inaccurate because our thoughts are foolish, but the slovenliness of our language makes it easier to have foolish thoughts.

A significant lesson is emerging from the Watergate hearings, apart from those that the powerful violate laws, subvert the United States Constitution and scorn decent ethics. The testimony of the Watergate crowd demonstrates that a stock political language has evolved which makes it difficult for the powerful and the public alike even to think meaningfully about respect for laws, loyalty to the Constitution or to exercise moral sensibilities. The torrent of circumlocutions, mechanical verbal formulas, misplaced technical jargon, palliative expressions, euphemisms and inflated phraseology indicate that the brains both of speakers and listeners are being anesthetized or stunted. Critical meanings are barred from the beginning in a form of conceptual contraception. Insofar as we become addicted to the corrupt Watergate language it is nonsense to speak of political or moral responsibility and irresponsibility. Lacking mastery of clear, meaningful language deprives us of the basic equipment required of responsible people. As we abandon meaningful language in favor of blather, we become positively irresponsible to ourselves as well as to others. In listening to the Watergate witnesses it often is hard to tell whether they are merely dissemblers trying to paralyze the minds of others, self-deceivers who have crippled their own intelligences, or glib dolls whose characters remained undeveloped as their smartness grew.

Whatever the character of the Watergate witnesses, the hearings show that political language has degenerated since Orwell's warning that thought and language decline together. Seemingly more than before in American politics the English language is used not as an instrument for forming and expressing thought. It is used more to prevent, confuse and conceal thought. Thus we have grown accustomed to calling political lingo "rhetoric." This good word has been so debased to stand for anything from propaganda and nonsense to vicious lies. As the pseudo-language takes hold—*even in the process of our determined attempts to regenerate responsibility in political life*—it drags us further into chaotic conditions leading logically and inevitably to political nihilism.

In my opinion we have been so concerned with the *1984* aspects of Watergate—the spying, wiretapping and other "dirty tricks" (another euphemism that emerged from the hearings)—that we have overlooked something at least as important. If our political language, and therefore our public thinking, becomes so debauched that moral meanings can no longer be clearly expressed or understood, then all the gadgets, technology and techniques of Watergate will be unnecessary. We will have already slipped into a *1984* nightmare. A society that cannot speak or understand sense is condemned to live nonsensically. To put it in Washingtonspeak, clear political meanings and the higher political values that depend on them will have become "no longer operative." In plain language, we will have become a nation of politically nonresponsible imbeciles "speaking in tongues." Not the inspired Biblical kind but the spurious Watergate sort.

Personal morality inexpressible

Although there are varieties of Watergate talk, there is one quality common to the witnesses' ways of speaking, one very important thread connecting the apparently disparate linguistic styles. Except when they are accusing current enemies, e.g. Mitchell's calling Jeb Magruder's testimony that he (Mitchell) reviewed tapes and documents gained through illegal wiretaps and burglary "a palpable, damnable lie," their language permits no raising of questions of personal responsibility for unethical or criminal conduct on their part or by their colleagues. Issues of moral right and wrong are inexpressible in their lingo. When Senator Weicker asked Herbert Porter what was "the quality of his mind" (Washingtonspeak for "what were you thinking?") while he dealt in improper use of campaign funds, Porter paused, then replied, "Senator, I'm not a moral philosopher." In politics as in ethics what our language prevents us from articulating, it prevents us from thinking.

Although the words of the Watergate people indicate that Washingtonspeak is well on the way to becoming a language in which the whole matter of legality, as well as ethics, will also be inexpressible, it has not yet reached that perfect state. Speakers of this odd language must at present rest content with its power to make only *personal* responsibility for illegal acts impossible. Just as it would have been impossible in Periclean Athens to speak of the internal combustion engine, computers or atomic energy, so in Washingtonspeak personal moral responsibility does not exist. To be sure, illegal acts still exist in Watergate glossology, but in the linguistic process achieved so far, illegalities exist *sui generis*. They constitute a kind of unholy creation from nothing by no one.

Circumlocutions

Several dominant features of Washingtonspeak have been greatly exposed during the Watergate hearings.

Continued

Mr. Dean: The first meeting on this date, and the afternoon meeting which occurred on March 1, related to preparing the President for his forthcoming press conference. The President asked me a number of questions about the Gray nomination hearings and facts that had come out during these hearings. In particular, I can recall him stating that there should be no problem with the fact that I had received the FBI reports. He said that I was conducting an investigation for him and that it would be perfectly proper for the counsel to the President to have looked at these reports. I did not tell the President that I had not conducted an investigation for him because I assumed he was well aware of this fact and that the so-called Dean investigation was a public relations matter, and that frequently the President made reference in press conferences to things that never had, in fact, occurred.

Senator Montoya: Now, let's go into the statements made by the President—I have copies here. On August 29, 1972, the President made this statement:

In addition to that, within our own staff, under my direction, counsel to the President, Mr. Dean, has conducted a complete investigation of all leads which might involve any present members of the White House staff or anybody in the government. I can say categorically that his investigation indicates that no one in the White House staff, no one in this administration presently employed, was involved in this very bizarre incident.

Now, did you participate in that?

Mr. Dean: No, sir, not at all. I was totally unaware of it and do not know who did prepare that for the President.

Senator Montoya: Was the President telling the truth when he made that statement?

Mr. Dean: Well, as I said in my statement yesterday, I would have counseled the President against the statement and I cited the reasons why I would have counseled the President against the statement because of the knowledge I had as to the fact that documents had been destroyed that were incriminating to Mr. Haldeman; the fact that I had suspicions about other people's involvement.

As I said yesterday also, if that were to be a literal statement as to somebody being involved in the very particular incident which occurred on June 17, which, the way it reads, does not indicate that, but if it originally was designed to do that, that would have been a true statement.

Circumlocutions and convoluted language are among the foremost instruments of this language of nonresponsibility. Champion among the witnesses in this skill is the voluble Mr. Ehrlichman. His method was to confound critical questions put to him by blanketing them with intense barrages of grape-shot syntax. The Senators questioning him were given time limits and most of them were poor cross-examiners, an opinion confirmed by a recent survey conducted among prominent trial lawyers. Ehrlichman, therefore, as one of my acquaintances put it, "talked the bastards to death" with such phrases as "we (Dean, Mitchell and Ehrlichman) made an agreement to go out and develop additional information if we could." One may seek, compile, file, pursue, fabricate, conceal, alter, reveal and do other things regarding information. But how does one "develop" it? In a darkroom? A chemist's laboratory? Ehrlichman's language leaves us ignorant of precisely what the three men had agreed to do and therefore unable to assess its morality or legality. We would be left in this quandary even if, as Ehrlichman said of his associates and himself, "we gathered together to compare ignorances." How do you and I compare what I do not know with what you do not know? If I speak no Greek and you speak no Chinese, how do we compare these tongues? For a comparison to be achieved, someone must introduce knowledge. But then someone would know something, and Ehrlichman was asserting he and his associates knew nothing when they gathered together.

In reply to the question why he had approved Mr. Kalmbach's mission of raising money for the jailed Watergate burglars, Ehrlichman allowed that his approval was only "perfunctory" and given because "Mitchell had some interest in making sure the defendants were well defended." Does "perfunctory" mean Ehrlichman was not responsible? What was Mr. Mitchell's "interest"? Was the payment for a legal defense, was it hush money, or both? Because of Ehrlichman's verbal dexterity in tying up the English language, it is impossible to know from his testimony who was responsible for what. Events merely happened.

Although Ehrlichman was aggressively or defiantly blunt throughout much of his confrontation with the Senate Committee, he repeatedly became almost incomprehensibly loquacious when questioned about his responsibility and that of others he insisted are blameless. When asked about the allegation made by both Richard Helms and General Vernon Walters, formerly the two top men at the C.I.A., that Ehrlichman and Haldeman suggested that the agency ask the F.B.I. to limit its investigation into the "laundering" of Republican money in Mexico on the pretext that the F.B.I. would endanger some pretended agency operation in that country, Ehrlichman's diction became inscrutable:

> My recollection of that meeting is at considerable variance with General Walters in the general thrust and in the details. In point of fact, as I recall it, we informed Mr. Helms and General Walters that the meeting was held at the President's request for the reasons I stated. Mr. Haldeman said that the Watergate was an obvious important political issue and that the President had no alternative but to order a full allout F.B.I. investigation until he was satisfied that there was some specific area from which the F.B.I. should not probe for fear of leaks through the F.B.I. or dissociated and disconnected C.I.A. activities that had no bearing on Watergate.

Ehrlichman displayed extraordinary skill in surrounding an outrageous opinion with tortuous verbiage which gives it a coating of justification. Thus he glibly took the offensive when questioned about the burglary of Daniel Ellsberg's psychiatrist's office:

> I think if it is clearly understood that the President has the constitutional power to prevent the betrayal of national security secrets, as I understand he does, and that is well understood by the American people, and an episode like that is seen in that context, there shouldn't be any problem.

What "constitutional power"? Which "national security secrets"? By whose definition? "Well understood by the American people"? "There shouldn't be any problem"? Ehrlichman's crossfire of stock phrases sends us diving for cover, numbs our minds and almost makes us sorry the topic was raised.

Washingtonspeak circumlocution is virtually invulnerable. It smothers any counterattack with more circumlocution. The circumlocution gains strength over each attempt to pierce it with Hydra's ability instantly to replace any of its serpents' heads which is cut off with two others. Thus Ehrlichman first explained—in his fashion—the payment of cash to the captured Watergate burglars by saying, "John Mitchell felt very strongly that it was important to have good legal representation for these defendants for a number of reasons—for political reasons, but also because we had these civil damage suits that had been filed by the Democrats." When pressed about exactly what were the "political reasons," Ehrlichman set the Hydra-like prowess of circumlocution upon his questioners. "Well," he said, "just that if there were to be a trial and it were to

take place before the election, that obviously that trial would have some political impact and good representation was simply essential." By this time the numerous heads of Ehrlichman's verbal monster were overwhelming. No one on the Committee pursued the question any further.

Similarly, Ehrlichman's response to a query about whether he suspected Jeb Magruder's involvement in the Watergate cover-up and what he did about his suspicion was so convoluted as to be totally uninformative. Again no Senator challenged Ehrlichman's confounding statement that:

> There came a time when there was a feeling that, at least on my part, based on what Mr. Dean was telling me about the unraveling of this thing, that Mr. Magruder may have had some involvement, and that culminated in a meeting with the Attorney General (Mitchell) at the end of July, on the 31st of July, where Magruder was specifically discussed. But just where in there I acquired the information, I can't tell you. Any questions?

Resort to circumlocution was characteristic of others at key points when questions of someone's personal responsibility threatened to surface. Senator Inouye asked Mitchell a pointed question in plain English: "Have you ever considered whether it was fair to the American people to conspire to keep them from the true facts of this matter [of a series of illegal and unethical actions]?" In the words of the old calypso song, Mitchell's reply was clear as mud and it covered the ground. "Yes, I am sure," he said, "that the subject matter crossed my mind many, many times. But I do not believe now, I did not believe then, that the President should be charged with the transgressions of others. And it is just as simple as that." The habit of using inflated blather at crucial points is so strong that John Dean's "I was trying to test the chronology of my knowledge" was typical.

The stock phrase

Another feature of the Watergate language of nonresponsibility is the use of stupefying stock phrases. A private meeting with the President of the United States arouses considerable interest about possibly revealing statements. But John Dean's "one on one with the President" sounds as impersonal as the shuffling of a deck of cards. It is mechanical in connotation, as are other phrases used by Watergate witnesses. They did not approve things but "signed off on them" as when Jeb Magruder said Mitchell signed off on a proposed project. The phrase makes Mitchell appear to casually flip a switch rather than consciously and knowingly make a decision. You, I and most people take orders from our bosses or superiors in our jobs or careers. John Dean "followed a channel of reporting." It sounds more prescribed by circumstances than an act of conscious obedience. The course of a channel is fixed and a good harbor pilot merely

Continued

John Kenneth Galbraith coined the term "wordfact" to describe the government's technique for distorting reality. It is one of the most subtle forms of propaganda. Here is his definition:

Wordfact

The wordfact makes words a precise substitute for reality. This is an enormous convenience. It means that to say something exists is a substitute for its existence. And to say that something will happen is as good as having it happen. The saving in energy is nearly total.

. . . Where once it was said of a statesman that he suited action to the words, now he suits the words to the action. If past action (or inaction) has failed to produce the desired results, then, by resort to wordfact, he quickly establishes that the undesired result was more desirable than the desired result.

John Kenneth Galbraith

Search today's newspaper for examples of the use of wordfact in both major and minor governmental announcements. Paste your clippings on this page.

Write a brief discussion of the difference between wordfact and a genuine event. Analyze two of your clippings, showing how you recognized them as examples of wordfact.

follows it. And reporting evokes much less responsibility than giving and taking instructions.

Watergate people never reflect on the past since such an activity would imply that they are capable of understanding elementaries of personal responsibility. They are forever "in hindsight" like so many creatures with eyes imbedded in their behinds. Thus they merely "see" the past in a manner that permits them not to commit themselves about their moral or legal culpability then or their present view whether they were responsible. For example in the following exchange with Samuel Dash, John Mitchell really reveals nothing about his responsibility for past behavior or his current opinion about that responsibility:

> Dash: "As Attorney General of the United States, why didn't you throw Mr. Liddy out of your office?"
> Mitchell: "Well, I think, Mr. Dash, in hindsight I not only should have thrown him out of the office, I should have thrown him out of the window."
> Dash: "Well, since you did neither, why didn't you at least recommend that Mr. Liddy be fired?"
> Mitchell: "Well, in hindsight, I probably should have done that too."

To describe a series of circumstances surrounding an event implies personal knowledge which in turn might imply personal responsibility. Therefore, Mitchell volunteered—after being asked a direct question regarding a suspicious meeting—"let me play out the scenario for you." He merely starts the movie projector but has no relation to what might appear on the screen.

Incidentally, whereas most people are told of criminal events, thereby raising questions of their complicity after the fact, Watergate people were merely "brought up to speed on" them. After all, the highway signs specify minimum as well as maximum legal speeds, right?

The stock phrase most used during the Watergate hearings was "at this point in time" and its variations, e.g. "at that point in time." At first these expressions sound merely like pretentious, elaborate ways of saying, "then," "now," "at that time," "at this time," etc. But the stock phrases are much more useful. "At that point in time" serves to isolate the event being discussed, to detach it, bracket it and set it apart from all other events and people. It becomes a moment existing by itself. Questionable conduct is thereby voided by being reduced to a mathematical point, a fiction having no dimensions, connections, history or relation to the present. Surgeons prefer to operate in a "clean field" established by isolation of the area of incision through elaborate operating room techniques. Only a swatch of flesh is presented to the surgeon's eyes instead of a whole patient. The surgeon is thus spared the unnerving sight of the patient's face, posture, and general human appearance at the critical time of surgery. "At that point of time" accomplishes an

Continued

analogous effect. The difference of course is that the surgical procedure serves a legitimate medical purpose, while the Watergate linguistic procedure obscures personal political and moral responsibility. Two of the axiomatic requirements of personal responsibility are motives before the deed and awareness of consequences after the deed. "At that point in time" foils both.

"Pre-situation" and "post-situation" are Watergate phrases which once again sever events from relations, connections, and hence responsibility. They are even more bloodless than the ordinary legal phrases "before the event" and "after the event."

But perhaps the most blatantly robot evoking phrase is John Dean's saying he "dealt with people telephonically." Now, when you call someone on the telephone, or he calls, and you and he talk, human behavior occurs and ordinary responsibilities for it become discussable. But no more comes to mind when one person deals with another telephonically than when we watch the whir of computer machinery. It is totally impersonal, mechanical, inhuman.

Specialized jargon

Another prominent feature of Watergate talk is the frequent misuse of technical jargon taken from specialized areas of life. Jargon used by specialists in reference to their speciality is meaningful and useful. It facilitates communication between the specialists whether it be in football, medicine, seamanship, stock brokerage, etc. But when appropriated for use in politics, technical jargon from other fields serves contrary purposes. Codes produced by misplaced jargon used in politics serve to mask the true nature of what is happening. And the use of jargon which is elsewhere legitimate lends an aura of justification and respectability to morally and legally dubious behavior. The use of appropriated jargon also serves the old priesthood mystique function of jargon. Those privy to the code enjoy a special, privileged, sophisticated status making them superior to us ordinary slobs.

Much of the jargon used by the Watergate people is taken from the fields of police work and cloak-and-dagger activity. The first is a legitimate profession, the second at least is glamorously mysterious. Unethical and illegal conduct becomes dressed up by the borrowed jargon. Thus, those engaged in burglary, malfeasance of office, criminal conspiracy and other evil conduct did not do these things over ordinary periods of time. They functioned "within time frames," a mechanically detached expression legitimately used in the computer field. Illegal domestic spies constitute a "new intelligence unit" and their equipment was said to need "housing," i.e. quarters that do not call attention to themselves. Images of Humphrey Bogart in trenchcoat playing cat and mouse with the Nazis instead of a sleazy group spying on the personal lives of law-abiding fellow Americans.

Illegal activity is spoken of as "games." Criminal conspiracy becomes a "game plan." Conspirators are "team players" like so many good halfbacks or third basemen. Thus Caulfield is said to have told McCord he was "fouling up the game plan." And Herbert Porter said he remained silent about nefarious doings at Nixon's campaign headquarters because he wanted to be a "team player." Criminal wiretappers are spoken of as "wire men," mere technicians like electricians legitimately used by the telephone company or police department.

Another linguistic style heavily favored by Watergate witnesses is the use of the passive rather than active voice. For example, instead of saying "I was curious" or "I thought of it," the witnesses have an infuriating habit of saying things like "it pricked my curiosity," "it crossed my mind," "it dawned on me." The effect of the habitual use of the passive voice is to create an illusory animistic world where events have lives, wills, motives and actions of their own without any human being responsible for them. This effect is enhanced by another tendency of the speakers—the constant use of multi-syllabic words when ordinary shorter ones would do. This old pedant's trick serves to numb independent thought in the listener and speaker. It also puffs up the status of the speaker in the minds of his audience and in his own self-esteem. Thus, the elegant lingo prettifies the sordid facts probably even in the minds of the guilty.

The use of martyred metaphors, similes and euphemisms serves the same function of obscuring import and responsibility from the guilty, from the victims and from bystanders. Illegally obtained or illegally used money is "laundered." Cleanliness is next to Godliness. Liddy's lengthy presentation to Mitchell, Dean and others of monstrous plans to use "mugging squads," kidnapping teams, compromising prostitutes and electronic eavesdropping against the White House's political opposition is described by use of a kindergarten phrase as a "show-and-tell session." The exposing of criminal involvement is spoken of as "this matter is starting to unravel." Presumably the journalists, Judge Sirica and the Senators and Congressmen searching out the truth are guilty of taking apart a neatly knitted sweater. Haldeman's reference to the exposition makes the obstruction of justice sound even more benign, and those uncovering it as naughty children or semi-vandals. According to Dean, the White House chief of staff said, "Once the toothpaste is out of the tube, it's going to be very hard to get it back in." Spank the brats playing with the tube!

Those who are spied upon by wiretaps are not referred to as subjects, and certainly not as victims. They were called "targets." Subjects and victims have rights, feelings, dignity—they are humans, citizens. But targets are inanimate things whose sole function is to be hit. Should one object? Do targets at a rifle or archery range complain? Don't be absurd.

Dean described a reassuring phone call from President Nixon as a "stroking session." Normally we stroke our lovers, children and pets—loving gestures, thoughts of which stimulate warm feelings in us. Was or was not Dean implying Nixon's complicity by use of this sensual metaphor? Poets use metaphors and similes to heighten meanings. Watergate people use them to blur meanings.

Among the most infuriating euphemisms used by Watergate witnesses is "surreptitious entry," meaning burglary. Thus a crime becomes a game of hide and seek, or at most a naughty prank. Next time you find a burglar in your home don't shout "police." Say "Oh, you surreptitious devil you!"

What ordinary crooks call "casing the joint" before a burglary is called by the Watergate bunch "a vulnerability and feasibility study." Surely these men were just students and technicians. But criminals? Never.

Illegal wiretapping is evil. Therefore the Watergate people engaged in "electronic surveillance." Spying on a person's activities is "visual surveillance." Evil people cover up, lie and bribe. Watergate people "contain situations" like so many protective dams.

Is this concern with language mere pedantry, a case of academic vanity? I suggest not. When an elaborate language of non-responsibility becomes current in the federal government, it would be irresponsible for us not to expose and correct it. We have been had. A language of non-responsibility is being forced upon us to describe a list of crimes, as Washingtonspeak would have it, "at the very highest levels" of the United States Government. It is a list which beggars our conscience when we push aside the elaborate Watergate talk camouflaging it. As Senator Weicker recently stated them, they should be sobering enough to bring us to our linguistic senses:

Conspiracy to commit breaking and entering.
Conspiracy to commit burglary.
Breaking and entering.
Burglary.
Conspiracy to obstruct justice.
Conspiracy to intercept wire or oral communications.
Perjury.
Subordination of perjury.
Conspiracy to obstruct a criminal investigation.
Conspiracy to destroy evidence.
Conspiracy to file false sworn statements.
Misprison of a felony.
Filing of false statements.
Interception of wire and oral communications.
Obstruction of criminal investigation.
Attempted interference with the administration of the Internal Revenue laws.
Attempted unauthorized use of Internal Revenue information.
To these we might add illegal use of the C.I.A., and

numerous unethical practices from violation of the doctor-patient privilege to sabotage of a presidential campaign.

An ancient Roman saying has it that the mind is dyed by the color of its thoughts. Since thoughts are formed in language, it follows that the mind is dyed by the tint of language. Could it be that so much outrageous conduct occurred at least in part because too many minds functioned through a language which extracted personal responsibility from consideration? Did addiction to Washingtonspeak facilitate the commission of conduct ordinarily considered unacceptable to the community at large?

It is time to cleanse our minds—and I don't mean launder—from the muck of Washingtonspeak if we still value government of responsible people, by responsible people and for responsible people. Although a more humble goal, this would be preferable to Mr. Haldeman's "zero-defect system."

Language is the dress of thought.
Samuel Johnson

Doubletalk

MY SERMON ON THE MEANING OF THE MANNA IN THE WILDERNESS CAN BE ADAPTED TO ALMOST ANY OCCASION, JOYFUL, OR, AS IN THE PRESENT CASE, DISTRESSING. I HAVE PREACHED IT AT HARVEST CELEBRATIONS, CHRISTENINGS, CONFIRMATIONS, ON DAYS OF HUMILIATION AND FESTAL DAYS.

Rev. C Chasuble, D.D., in *The Importance of Being Earnest* by Oscar Wilde

LET THE LANGUAGE BE AMBIGUOUS ENOUGH THAT IF THE TEXT BE SUCCESSFULLY CARRIED OUT, ALL CREDIT MAY BE CLAIMED, BUT IF THE TEXT BE UNSUCCESSFULLY CARRIED OUT, A TECHNICAL ALIBI CAN BE SET UP OUT OF THE TEXT ITSELF.

Business executive quoted in *Fortune*

It would be premature to pass any final judgment on this development	❯	*We don't know yet*
One may detect an underlying contradiction between outward form and reality	❯	*It's a fake*
The new weapons system is encountering serious technical difficulties at a late stage in its development, mainly because of its extreme sophistication	❯	*One more big bill will have to be paid for an arms flop*
National independent nuclear deterrent with long-range delivery capability	❯	*Homemade pie in the sky*

Have you ever tried talking to your gas and electric company?

Man bites PG&E

Berkeley author (and Co-op member) Theodore Roszak has undertaken what he calls a "flea bite tactic" in the paying of his monthly PG&E bill. Along with his check, he sends an "important notice" informing that utility that what with one thing and another he is decreasing his monthly payments by 10 percent.

In a note to the Co-op News, Roszak said, "From now until we municipalize PG&E, I will be sending the following message to everybody's favorite utility each month with my steadily escalating bill. Perhaps others would care to do the same." Here is the Roszak notice:

IMPORTANT NOTICE

We regret to inform you that, due to the extraordinary rise in our costs of necessary supplies and services over the past twenty-four months, we will be forced at this time to decrease our monthly payments to PG&E by ten percent.

We know you must understand how severely the inflationary pressures of recent years have increased the expense of our daily survival. In spite of the steady upward spiral in our costs of consumption, this is the *first time* in the history of our relations with PG&E that we have decreased our monthly rates.

Now, however, in the unprecedented crisis that confronts our nation's consuming public, we have no choice but to shift a small portion of these heavy costs to those, like PG&E's shareholders, who are better able to absorb them with a minimum effect upon their standard of living.

As we are sure you realize, the consuming public is a vital sector of our free enterprise economy. Its capacity to survive and spend is of the greatest importance to our national interest. We know, therefore, that you will bear with us during this difficult period, in the full knowledge that we intend to continue our loyal patronage of PG&E and to make prompt payment of your bills at our new lower rates. THANK YOU.

 Write a similar response to a bureaucratic announcement you have read.

How would you sell yourself for a job?

Real-estate want ads in the Sunday newspapers often list "open houses," and provide descriptions of these houses for sale. Clip out three or four of these ads for "open houses" that are near your neighborhood; then visit them. Compare the descriptions in the ads with what you see. Make up your own Home Buyers' Guide.

HOME BUYER'S GUIDE

The real-estate man told us that now is the time to buy a house. This month only, but maybe next month too, it is possible to buy a $25,000 house for just $45,000. The man said that by December $25,000 houses will be going for $55,000, so we had better act quick, quick, quick. We didn't but we learned a little.

We learned that most real-estate agents advertise in code. I have cracked this code by driving around the countryside and looking into houses for sale—an ingenious method devised by British cryptographers late in World War II.

I can now offer a handy corrective to the language in the classified ads by revealing how the secret real-estate code works.

Victorian: drafty

Colonial: built prior to the second Eisenhower Administration

Gracious colonial: you can't afford it

Leisure home: habitable during July and August

Ranch: egg box wearing a cowboy hat

Raised ranch: ranch set on a slope

Chalet: ranch set on a steep slope

Older home: lists disconcertingly to the southwest

Comfortable: small

Cozy: teeny-weeny

Cute: itsy-bitsy

Immaculate: kitchen walls are not as greasy as the pit floor at Ralph's Texaco

Patio: spot near back door where cement truck overturned

Piazza: porch

Gleaming bathroom: bathroom

Vanity bathroom: bathroom with a table nailed to the wall

Carriage house: garage leaning against '48 Dodge

Convenient to shopping: bay window overlooks an A&P parking lot

$300 to heat: $780 to heat

Family room: basement with 100-watt light bulb

Needs some fixing up: leg of bathtub protruding through kitchen ceiling needs polishing

Brook crosses property: by way of the cellar

Raised-hearth fireplace: has a little chair that the fire can sit on

Desirable corner: corner

Entrance foyer: door

Many extras: recent owners left behind rags, coat hangers, mysterious wire running from back door to bathtub, half a bottle of cough syrup

Low taxes: fire department requires bribes

Nice neighborhood: and let's keep it that way!

Heritage estate setting: (this description continues to baffle the world's ace cryptographers)

Only 15 minutes from . . .: only 40 minutes from . . .

Seeing is believing: seeing is believing

Make an offer: say something amusing

Richard Lipez, Lanesboro, Mass.

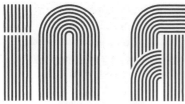

IN ART

PROPAGANDA

Sometimes propaganda looks like something else. It's easily recognized in an advertisement, or an appeal for funds, or a call for political action. But it can take many other forms as well.

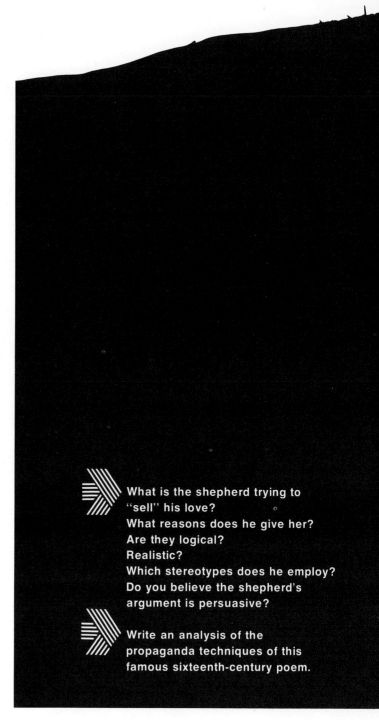

What is the shepherd trying to "sell" his love?
What reasons does he give her?
Are they logical?
Realistic?
Which stereotypes does he employ?
Do you believe the shepherd's argument is persuasive?

Write an analysis of the propaganda techniques of this famous sixteenth-century poem.

The Passionate Shepherd to His Love

Come live with me and be my Love,
And we will all the pleasures prove
That hills and valleys, dales and fields,
Or woods or steepy mountain yields.

And we will sit upon the rocks,
And see the shepherds feed their flocks
By shallow rivers, to whose falls
Melodious birds sing madrigals.

And I will make thee beds of roses
And a thousand fragrant posies;
A cap of flowers, and a kirtle
Embroidered all with leaves of myrtle;

A gown made of the finest wool
Which from our pretty lambs we pull;
Fair-linéd slippers for the cold,
With buckles of the purest gold;

A belt of straw and ivy buds
With coral clasps and amber studs—
And if these pleasures may thee move,
Come live with me and be my Love.

The shepherd swains shall dance and sing
For thy delight each May morning—
If these delights thy mind may move,
Then live with me and be my Love.

Christopher Marlowe, 1564–1593

The Nymph's Reply to the Shepherd

If all the world and love were young
And truth in every shepherd's tongue,
These pretty pleasures might me move
To live with thee and be thy love.

Time drives the flocks from field to fold
When rivers rage and rocks grow cold,
And Philomel becometh dumb;
The rest complain of cares to come.

The flowers do fade, and wanton fields
To wayward winter reckoning yields;
A honey tongue, a heart of gall,
Is fancy's spring, but sorrow's fall.

Thy gowns, thy shoes, thy beds of roses,
Thy cap, thy kirtle, and thy posies
Soon break, soon wither, soon forgotten,
In folly ripe, in reason rotten.

Thy belt of straw and ivy buds,
Thy coral clasps and amber studs,
All these in me no means can move
To come to thee and be thy love.

But could youth last and love still breed,
Had joys no date nor age no need,
Then these delights my mind might move
To live with thee and be thy love.

Sir Walter Raleigh, 1552–1618

Propaganda in poetry . . .

Read the following poems which were written in several different periods. Discuss them with your classmates, considering the purpose of each and the persuasive methods used by the poets. Note your conclusions about the effectiveness of poetry as propaganda.

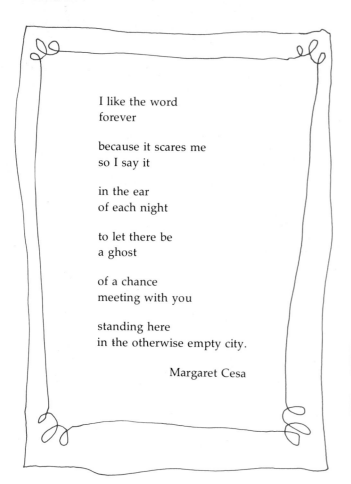

I like the word
forever

because it scares me
so I say it

in the ear
of each night

to let there be
a ghost

of a chance
meeting with you

standing here
in the otherwise empty city.

Margaret Cesa

Canticle

The sharks tooth is perfect for biting. The intent
matters./ I am sick of beautiful things
/ and I would make a robe of gestures

without beauty except for the beauty inherent
in words and motion.

Listen/ Listen/ listen/ Listen/ Listen

to the words as waves/ pressures
all is destruction—without it there is
no strength.   The muscle builds
itself double   by destruction of cells.

The tendons whisper to the skeleton

Listen/ Listen/ listen/ Listen/ Listen
and only the nerves hear.
The field and seed are one thing destroying
the other. Intent, enwrapped with one another

Erethism is love. Love

Inventing a thing of leaves and flowers

'retractions devour' the thing burgeoning
is the thing intent/ Love/ Strength/ Light
and Dark/ spring to blossoms.

Michael McClure

Poem

For years I've heard
others speak like birds.
                    The words
clicking.
          One day I spoke
articulate
          the words *tic-ed*
in my throat.
                    It was
as if love woke
                    after anger.
The words
          sure—
                    Listen.
(*CHURRR*)
          Love wakes
at the breakfast table.
                    (*CHURRR*)
Not that
          the language itself has wings.
(*CHURRR*)   Not that
                    (*CHURRR*)
unfortunate skill.
                    Listen.
The words
          sure as a scream.

                    Robin Blaser

We Wear the Mask

We wear the mask that grins and lies,
It hides our cheeks and shades our eyes—
This debt we pay to human guile;
With torn and bleeding hearts we smile,
And mouth with myriad subtleties
Why should the world be otherwise,
In counting all our tears and sighs?

Nay, let them only see us while
   We wear the mask.

We smile, but, O great Christ, our cries
To thee from tortured souls arise.
We sing, but oh the clay is vile
Beneath our feet, and long the mile;
But let the world dream otherwise,
   We wear the mask.

                    Paul Laurence Dunbar

Psalm 150

Praise ye the Lord.
Praise God in his sanctuary:
praise him in the firmament of his power.
2 Praise him for his mighty acts:
praise him according to his excellent greatness.
3 Praise him with the sound of the trumpet:
praise him with the psaltery and harp.
4 Praise him with the timbrel and dance:
praise him with stringed instruments and organs.
5 Praise him upon the loud cymbals:
praise him upon the high sounding cymbals.
6 Let every thing that hath breath praise the Lord.
Praise ye the Lord.

The World Is Too Much With Us

The world is too much with us; late and soon,
Getting and spending, we lay waste our powers:
Little we see in Nature that is ours;
We have given our hearts away, a sordid boon!
The sea that bares her bosom to the moon;
The winds that will be howling at all hours,
And are up-gathered now like sleeping flowers;
For this, for everything, we are out of tune;
It moves us not.—Great God! I'd rather be
A Pagan suckled in a creed outworn;
So might I, standing on this pleasant lea,
Have glimpses that would make me less forlorn;
Have sight of Proteus rising from the sea;
Or hear old Triton blow his wreathéd horn.
(1806; 1807)

William Wordsworth

Karma

Christmas was in the air and all was well
With him, but for a few confusing flaws
In divers of God's images. Because
A friend of his would neither buy nor sell,
Was he to answer for the axe that fell?
He pondered; and the reason for it was,
Partly, a slowly freezing Santa Claus
Upon the corner, with his beard and bell.
Acknowledging an improvident surprise,
He magnified a fancy that he wished
The friend whom he had wrecked were here again.
Not sure of that, he found a compromise;
And from the fullness of his heart he fished
A dime for Jesus who had died for man.

Edwin Arlington Robinson

Write a short poem designed to persuade your reader to do something, or believe something, or feel something, or even to buy something. Ask your classmates to consider its effectiveness as propaganda.

The following short story, based on legend, has a clear message, but the author never states it. Write the message in a short, simple sentence, as though it were a proverb.

_____

_____

_____

_____

The Phoenix

Lord Strawberry, a nobleman, collected birds. He had the finest aviary in Europe, so large that eagles did not find it uncomfortable, so well laid out that both humming-birds and snow-buntings had a climate that suited them perfectly. But for many years the finest set of apartments remained empty, with just a label saying: "PHOENIX. *Habitat: Arabia.*"

Many authorities on bird life had assured Lord Strawberry that the phoenix is a fabulous bird, or that the breed was long extinct. Lord Strawberry was unconvinced: his family had always believed in phoenixes. At intervals he received from his agents (together with statements of their expenses) birds which they declared were the phoenix but which turned out to be orioles, macaws, turkey buzzards dyed orange, etc., or stuffed cross-breeds, ingeniously assembled from various plumages. Finally Lord Strawberry went himself to Arabia, where, after some months, he found a phoenix, won its confidence, caught it, and brought it home in perfect condition.

It was a remarkably fine phoenix, with a charming character—affable

to the other birds in the aviary and much attached to Lord Strawberry. On its arrival in England it made a great stir among ornithologists, journalists, poets, and milliners, and was constantly visited. But it was not puffed by these attentions, and when it was no longer in the news, and the visits fell off, it showed no pique or rancour. It ate well, and seemed perfectly contented.

It costs a great deal of money to keep up an aviary. When Lord Strawberry died he died penniless. The aviary came on the market. In normal times the rarer birds, and certainly the phoenix, would have been bid for by the trustees of Europe's great zoological societies, or by private persons in the U.S.A.; but as it happened Lord Strawberry died just after a world war, when both money and bird-seed were hard to come by, indeed the cost of bird-seed was one of the things which had ruined Lord Strawberry. The London *Times* urged in a leader that the phoenix be bought for the London Zoo, saying that a nation of bird-lovers had a moral right to own such a rarity; and a fund, called the Strawberry Phoenix Fund, was opened. Students, naturalists, and school-children contributed according to their means; but their means were small, and there were no large donations. So Lord Strawberry's executors (who had the death duties to consider) closed with the higher offer of Mr. Tancred Poldero, owner and proprietor of Poldero's Wizard Wonderworld.

For quite a while Mr. Poldero considered his phoenix a bargain. It was a civil and obliging bird, and adapted itself readily to its new surroundings. It did not cost much to feed, it did not

Continued

mind children; and though it had no tricks, Mr. Poldero supposed it would soon pick up some. The publicity of the Strawberry Phoenix Fund was now most helpful. Almost every contributor now saved up another half-crown in order to see the phoenix. Others, who had not contributed to the fund, even paid double to look at it on the five-shilling days.

But then business slackened. The phoenix was as handsome as ever, and as amiable; but, as Mr. Poldero said, it hadn't got Udge. Even at popular prices the phoenix was not really popular. It was too quiet, too classical. So people went instead to watch the antics of the baboons, or to admire the crocodile who had eaten the woman.

One day Mr. Poldero said to his manager, Mr. Ramkin:

"How long since any fool paid to look at the phoenix?"

"Matter of three weeks," replied Mr. Ramkin.

"Eating his head off," said Mr. Poldero. "Let alone the insurance. Seven shillings a week it costs me to insure that bird, and I might as well insure the Archbishop of Canterbury."

"The public don't like him. He's too quiet for them, that's the trouble. Won't mate nor nothing. And I've tried him with no end of pretty pollies, ospreys, and Cochin-Chinas, and the Lord knows what. But he won't look at them."

"Wonder if we could swap him for a livelier one," said Mr. Poldero.

"Impossible. There's only one of him at a time."

"Go on!"

"I mean it. Haven't you ever read what it says on the label?"

They went to the phoenix's cage. It flapped its wings politely, but they paid no attention. They read:

"**Pansy.** *Phoenix phoenixissima formosissima arabiana.* This rare and fabulous bird is **unique.** The World's Old Bachelor. Has no mate and doesn't want one. When old, sets fire to itself and emerges miraculously reborn. Specially imported from the East."

"I've got an idea," said Mr. Poldero. "How old do you suppose that bird is?"

"Looks in its prime to me," said Mr. Ramkin.

"Suppose," continued Mr. Poldero, "we could somehow get him alight? We'd advertise it beforehand, of course, work up interest. Then we'd have a new bird, and a bird with some romance about it, a bird with a life-story. We could sell a bird like that."

Mr. Ramkin nodded.

"I've read about it in a book." he said. "You've got to give them scented woods and what not, and they build a nest and sit down on it and catch fire spontaneous. But they won't do it till they're old. That's the snag."

"Leave that to me." said Mr. Poldero. "You get those scented woods, and I'll do the ageing."

It was not easy to age the phoenix. Its allowance of food was halved, and halved again, but though it grew thinner its eyes were undimmed and its plumage glossy as ever. The heating was turned off; but it puffed out its feathers against the cold, and seemed none the worse. Other birds were put into its cage, birds of a peevish and quarrelsome nature. They pecked and chivied it; but the phoenix

was so civil and amiable that after a day or two they lost their animosity. Then Mr. Poldero tried alley cats. These could not be won by manners, but the phoenix darted above their heads and flapped its golden wings in their faces, and daunted them.

Mr. Poldero turned to a book on Arabia, and read that the climate was dry. "Aha!" said he. The phoenix was moved to a small cage that had a sprinkler in the ceiling. Every night the sprinkler was turned on. The phoenix began to cough. Mr. Poldero had another good idea. Daily he stationed himself in front of the cage to jeer at the bird and abuse it.

When spring was come, Mr. Poldero felt justified in beginning a publicity campaign about the ageing phoenix. The old public favourite, he said, was nearing its end. Meanwhile he tested the bird's reactions every

few days by putting a few tufts of foul-smelling straw and some strands of rusty barbed wire into the cage, to see if it were interested in nesting yet. One day the phoenix began turning over the straw. Mr. Poldero signed a contract for the film rights. At last the hour seemed ripe. It was a fine Saturday evening in May. For some weeks the public interest in the ageing phoenix had been working up, and the admission charge had risen to five shillings. The enclosure was thronged. The lights and the cameras were trained on the cage, and a loud-speaker proclaimed to the audience the rarity of what was about to take place.

"The phoenix," said the loud-speaker, "is the aristocrat of bird-life. Only the rarest and most expensive specimens of oriental wood, drenched in exotic perfumes, will tempt him to construct his strange love-nest."

Now a neat assortment of twigs and shavings, strongly scented, was shoved into the cage.

"The phoenix," the loud-speaker continued, "is as capricious as Cleopatra, as luxurious as la du Barry, as heady as a strain of wild gypsy music. All the fantastic pomp and passion of the ancient East, its languorous magic, its subtle cruelties . . ."

"Lawks!" cried a woman in the crowd. "He's at it!"

A quiver stirred the dulled plumage. The phoenix turned its head from side to side. It descended, staggering, from its perch. Then wearily it began to pull about the twigs and shavings.

The cameras clicked, the lights blazed full on the cage. Rushing to the loud-speaker, Mr. Poldero exclaimed:

"Ladies and gentlemen, this is the thrilling moment the world has breathlessly awaited. The legend of cen-turies is materializing before our modern eyes. The phoenix . . ."

The phoenix settled on its pyre and appeared to fall asleep.

The film director said:

"Well, if it doesn't evaluate more than this, mark instructional."

At that momemt the phoenix and the pyre burst into flames. The flames streamed upwards, leaping out on every side. In a minute or two everything was burned to ashes, and some thousand people, including Mr. Poldero, perished in the blaze.

Sylvia Townsend Warner

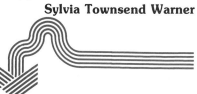

Would you classify "The Phoenix" as propaganda? Justify your classification in a single paragraph.

Persuaders with a celluloid weapon . . .

It's possible that television viewing, with all its breaks and cuts, and the inattention, except for action, and spinning the dial to find some action, is partly responsible for destruction of the narrative sense—that delight in following a story through its complications to its conclusion, which is perhaps a child's first conscious artistic pleasure. The old staples of entertainment—inoffensive genres like the adventure story or the musical or the ghost story or the detective story—are no longer commercially safe for moviemakers, and it may be that audiences don't have much more than a TV span of attention left: they want to be turned on and they spend most of their time turning off. Something similar and related may be happening in reading tastes and habits: teen-agers that I meet have often read Salinger and some Orwell and *Lord of the Flies* and some Joyce Cary and sometimes even Dostoyevsky, but they are not interested in the "classic" English novels of Scott or Dickens, and what is more to the point, they don't read the Sherlock Holmes stories or even the modern detective fiction that in the thirties and forties was an accepted part of the shared experience of adolescents. Whatever the reasons —and they must be more than TV, they must have to do with modern life and the sense of urgency it produces—audiences can no longer be depended on to respond to conventional forms.

Perhaps they prefer incoherent,

meaningless movies because they are not required to remember or connect. They can feel superior, contemptuous—as they do toward television advertising. Even when it's a virtuoso triumph, the audience is contemptuous toward advertising, because, after all, they see through it—they know somebody is trying to sell something.

It has become easy—especially for those who consider "time" a problem and a great theme—to believe that fast editing, out of normal sequence, which makes it difficult, or impossible, for the audience to know if any action is taking place, is somehow more "cinematic" than a consecutively told story. For a half century movies have, when necessary, shifted action in time and place and the directors generally didn't think it necessary to slap us in the face with each cut or to call out, "Look what I can do!" Yet people who should know better will tell you how "cinematic" *The Loneliness of the Long Distance Runner* or *This Sporting Life* is—as if fiddling with the time sequence was good in itself, proof that the "medium" is really being used. Perhaps, after a few decades of indoctrination in high art, they are convinced that a movie is cinematic when they don't understand what's going on.

Pauline Kael

What do you think about Pauline Kael's ideas? Weave your thoughts into an essay.

"The cinema camera is the agent of Democracy," wrote D. W. Griffith in 1917. "It levels barriers between races and classes." What Griffith perceived, as have all makers of message films in the silent and sound eras, is the potential of the film medium for social education as well as diversion. Recognizing the necessity to first stir men's hearts in order to change their attitudes, Hollywood message-filmmakers have utilized the entertainment *story* film as a vehicle for expressing a social viewpoint. By couching their social comment within an emotion-involving dramatic story, these filmmakers have been instinctively aware that to "teach" and persuade mass audiences, a movie must first engage and hold their attention.

Persuaders armed with the celluloid weapon have dealt with the entire spectrum of problems and issues endemic to American

In the Soviet Union the popular arts are in the service of the state and are recognized as creative forces; they condition people to be good by the Soviet standard of goodness. We maintain that this results in slavery, which is approximately what they think of our system. The grain of truth we can get from the Soviet critics is important: they see that our mass media do have a creative effect on our lives. That they do not like the effect is of small consequence.

Gilbert Seldes

society. For almost seventy years the American message film has explored such social problems as racial and ethnic prejudice, drug addiction, alcoholism, labor inequities, penal inhumanity, crime and juvenile delinquency, corruption in politics and government, and that most cancerous of all social ills, war. Certainly all of these problems have existed throughout most of America's history, but in the twentieth century they seem more demanding of public attention and solution. Indeed, as these problems have become more acute and aggravated at certain crucial moments of the twentieth century, the message film has reflected the anxiety surrounding them. Because message films deal with social issues when they are most nagging and topical, and because the viewpoints they espouse are dependent on acceptance by large "paying" audiences, they have represented an important index to social thought in America since the turn of the century.

D. White and R. Averson

> *"The cinema camera*
>
> *is the agent*
>
> *of Democracy,"*

Movies manipulate emotions and values. Just as advertising can and does promote anxieties to increase consumption, movies may increase certain emotional needs which can then only be satisfied by more movies. In a time of change and conflict such as we experience today, movies and other mass communications emphasize and reinforce one set of values rather than another, present models for human relations through their portrayal by glamorous stars, and show life, truly or falsely, beyond the average individual's everyday experiences. . . .

Like all drama and literature, movies extend the experiences of the audience vicariously, and translate problems which are common to mankind into specific and personal situations, with which identification is easy. Results from such preliminary research with audience reactions provide the hypothesis that audiences tend to accept as true that part of a movie story which is beyond their experience.

Hortense Powdermaker

The noted anthropologist Hortense Powdermaker once described Hollywood as "the dream factory." It cannot be denied that Hollywood's studio assembly lines have fabricated escapist eyewash for more than three generations of Americans: lollipop boy-meets-girl dreams; dreams of mystery, adventure, and derring-do; dreams of fortunes effortlessly made and plush Everlasting Success. But not all dreams are merely personally gratifying wish fulfillments; there are some that reveal the collective fears and hopes of a society confronting its problems and striving for solutions. Hollywood has given audiences these dreams, too. How these "social dreams" have been expressed in a long and consistently vigorous tradition of the *message film* is essentially what this book is about.

Whether termed "message films," "problem films," or "films of social consciousness," such films indicate a recognition of the potential of motion pictures for more than diversion. Incorporating but going beyond the pleasure principle of mass entertainment, they utilize the film medium for expressing social commentary with the intention of drawing public attention to various social issues. They are purposely, and in the broadest meaning of the word, propaganda films; and their producers, directors, and writers can indeed be called social persuaders armed with a celluloid weapon.

D. White and R. Averson

To insure that we may gullibly accept the historic fallacy that our predecessors came here to create a "free" nation, history books, in conjunction with the makers of filmic history, have conveniently omitted telling us about the many indigenous tribes or nations exterminated on behalf of freedom. Hollywood has continued to perpetuate the myth by creating either (1) a noble red man, or (2) a vicious savage, both of whom deny the white man his proper Christian right to this continent.

No other race or culture depicted on film has been made to assume such a permanent fictional identity. So we cannot understand how the constant extermination of the Native American in films can possibly be analyzed in the same context with other misrepresented ethnic and racial minorities. After

all, these other maligned people are trespassers as well. The fact is that the "American Indian" is the only legitimate native of this land. Yet he is *racially*, not ethnically, isolated in our minds as *one minority*. He has been put on reservations apportioned to him on a vague tribal basis. Yet Hollywood has continued to be a co-conspirator in committing cultural genocide by subverting the Native American's various ethnic identities and retaining him as a racial scapegoat. By explicitly justifying the genocide perpetrated by our forefathers, Hollywood utilizes our ignorance to enforce our egotism.

Ralph and Natasha Friar

Some movies, such as *Mrs. Miniver, The Grapes of Wrath, Triumph of the Will*, have been made for obvious propaganda purposes, but is there a sense in which all movies contain elements of propaganda?
What do the movies tell us about

racial minorities
lawyers
doctors
women
sex
fashions
life styles
young people
college life
for example?

Think about a movie you have seen recently, and write a short analysis of the various facets of propaganda you noticed in it.

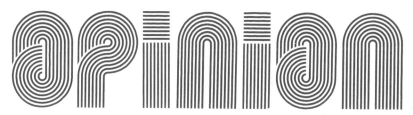

The following material reflects past and present bias toward minority groups.

Interview some Blacks, Chicanos, or Indians on your campus to discover whether they feel White attitudes and propaganda have really changed toward them in recent years. What evidence can they cite? Then list any changes that you have noticed in yourself, other people, and in the media. Compose an essay in which you bring together the findings gathered from your explorations.

I LIKE TO THINK OF
HARRIET TUBMAN

I like to think of Harriet Tubman.
Harriet Tubman who carried a revolver,
who had a scar on her head from a rock thrown
by a slave-master (because she
talked back), and who
had a ransom on her head
of thousands of dollars and who
was never caught, and who
had no use for the law
when the law was wrong,
who defied the law. I like
to think of her.
I like to think of her especially
when I think of the problem of
feeding children.

The legal answer
to the problem of feeding children
is ten free lunches every month,
being equal, in the child's real life,
to eating lunch every other day.
Monday but not Tuesday.
I like to think of the President
eating lunch Monday, but not
Tuesday.
And when I think of the President
and the law, and the problem of
feeding children, I like to
think of Harriet Tubman
and her revolver.

And then sometimes
I think of the President
and other men,
men who practise the law,
who revere the law,
who make the law,
who enforce the law,
who live behind
and operate through
and feed themselves
at the expense of
starving children
because of the law,
men who sit in paneled offices
and think about vacations
and tell women
whose care it is to feed children
not to be hysterical
not to be hysterical as in the word
hysterikos, the greek for
womb suffering,
not to suffer in their
wombs,
not to care,
not to bother the men
because they want to think
of other things
and do not want
to take the women seriously.

I want them
to take women seriously.
I want them to think about Harriet Tubman,
and remember,
remember she was beat by a white man
and she lived
and she lived to redress her grievances,
and she lived in swamps
and wore the clothes of a man
bringing hundreds of fugitives from
slavery, and was never caught,
and led an army,
and won a battle,
and defied the laws
because the laws were wrong, I want men
to take us seriously.
I am tired, wanting them to think
about right and wrong.
I want them to fear.
I want them to feel fear now
as I have felt suffering in the womb, and
I want them
to know
that there is always a time
there is always a time to make right
what is wrong,
there is always a time
for retribution
and that time
is beginning.

Susan Griffin

**Much of the propaganda about the relationships of various races and ethnic groups in America has been embodied in literature.
Here is an example written by a black author.**

THE WELCOME TABLE

for sister Clara Ward

I'm going to sit at the Welcome table
Shout my troubles over
Walk and talk with Jesus
Tell God how you treat me
One of these days!
—*Spiritual*

The old woman stood with eyes uplifted in her Sunday-go-to-meeting clothes: high shoes polished about the tops and toes, a long rusty dress adorned with an old corsage, long withered, and the remnants of an elegant silk scarf as headrag stained with grease from the many oily pigtails underneath. Perhaps she had known suffering. There was a dazed and sleepy look in her aged blue-brown eyes. But for those who searched hastily for "reasons" in that old tight face, shut now like an ancient door, there was nothing to be read. And so they gazed nakedly upon their own fear transferred; a fear of the black and the old, a terror of the unknown as well as of the deeply known. Some of those who saw her there on the church steps spoke words about her that were hardly fit to be heard, others held their pious peace; and some felt vague stirrings of pity, small and persistent and hazy, as if she were an old collie turned out to die.

She was angular and lean and the color of poor gray Georgia earth, beaten by king cotton and the extreme weather. Her elbows were wrinkled and thick, the skin ashen but durable, like the bark of old pines. On her face centuries were folded into the circles around one eye, while around the other, etched and mapped as if for print, ages more threatened again to live. Some of them there at the church saw the age, the dotage, the missing buttons down the front of her mildewed black dress. Others saw cooks, chauffeurs, maids, mistresses, children denied or smothered in the deferential way she held her cheek to the side, toward the ground. Many of them saw jungle orgies in an evil place, while others were reminded of riotous anarchists looting and raping in the streets. Those who knew the hesitant creeping up on them of the law, saw the beginning of the end of the sanctuary of Christian worship, saw the desecration of Holy Church, and saw an invasion of privacy, which they struggled to believe they still kept.

Still she had come down the road toward the big white church alone. Just herself, an old forgetful woman, nearly blind with age. Just her and her eyes raised dully to the glittering cross that crowned the sheer silver steeple. She had walked along the road in a stagger from her house a half mile away. Perspiration, cold and clammy, stood on her brow and along the creases by her thin wasted nose. She stopped to calm herself on the wide front steps, not looking about her as they might have expected her to do, but simply standing quite still, except for a slight quivering of her throat and tremors that shook her cotton-stockinged legs.

The reverend of the church stopped her pleasantly as she stepped into the vestibule. Did he say, as they thought he did, kindly, "Auntie, you know this is not your church?" As if one could choose the wrong one. But no one remembers, for they never spoke of it afterward, and she brushed past him anyway, as if she had been brushing past him all her life, except this time she was in a hurry. Inside the church she sat on the very first bench from the back, gazing with concentration at the stained-glass window over her head. It was cold, even inside the church, and she was shivering. Everybody could see. They stared at her as they came in and sat down near the front. It was cold, very cold to them, too; outside the church it was below freezing and not much above inside. But the sight of her, sitting here somehow passionately ignoring them, brought them up short, burning.

The young usher, never having turned anyone out of his church before, but not even considering this job as *that* (after all, she had no right to be there, certainly), went up to her and whispered that she should leave. Did he call her "Grandma," as later he seemed to recall he had? But for those who actually hear such traditional pleasantries and to whom they actually mean something, "Grandma" was not one, for she did not pay him any attention, just muttered, "Go 'way," in a weak sharp *bothered* voice, waving his frozen blond hair and eyes from near her face.

It was the ladies who finally did what to them had to be done. Daring their burly indecisive husbands to throw the old colored woman out they made their point. God, mother, country, earth, church. It involved all that, and well they knew it. Leather bagged and shoed, with good calfskin gloves to keep out the cold, they looked with contempt at the bloodless gray arthritic hands of the old woman, clenched loosely, restlessly in her lap. Could their husbands expect them to sit up in church with *that*? No, no, the husbands were quick to answer and even quicker to do their duty.

Under the old woman's arms they placed their hard fists (which afterwards smelled of decay and musk—the fermenting scent of onionskins and rotting greens). Under the old woman's arms they raised their fists, flexed their muscular shoulders, and out she flew through the door, back under the cold blue sky. This done, the wives folded their healthy arms across their trim middles and felt at once justified and scornful. But none of them said so, for none of them ever spoke of the incident again. Inside the church it was warmer. They sang, they prayed. The protection and promise of God's impartial love grew more not less desirable as the sermon gathered fury and lashed itself out above their penitent heads.

The old woman stood at the top of the steps looking about in bewilderment. She had been singing in her head. They had interrupted her. Promptly she began to sing again, though this time a sad song. Suddenly, however, she looked down the long gray highway and saw something interesting and delightful coming. She started to grin, toothlessly, with short giggles of joy, jumping about and slapping her hands on her knees. And soon it became apparent why she was so happy. For coming down the highway at a firm though leisurely pace was Jesus. He was wearing an immaculate white, long dress trimmed in gold around the neck and hem, and a red, a bright red, cape. Over his left arm he carried a brilliant blue blanket. He was wearing sandals and a beard and he had long brown hair parted on the right side. His eyes, brown, had wrinkles around them as if he smiled or looked at the sun a lot. She would have known him, recognized him, anywhere. There was a sad but joyful look to his face, like a candle was glowing behind it, and he walked with sure even steps in her direction, as if he were walking on the sea. Except that he was not carrying in his arms a baby sheep, he looked exactly like the picture of him that she had hanging over her bed at home. She had taken it out of a white lady's Bible while she was working for her. She had looked at that picture for more years than she could remember, but never once had she really expected to see him. She squinted her eyes to be sure he wasn't carrying a little sheep in one arm, but he was not. Ecstatically she began to wave her arms for fear he would miss seeing her, for he walked looking straight ahead on the shoulder of the highway, and from time to time looking upward at the sky.

All he said when he got up close to her was "Follow me," and she bounded down to his side with all the bob and speed of one so old. For every one of his long determined steps she made two quick ones. They walked along in deep silence for a long time. Finally she started telling him about how many years she had cooked for them, cleaned for them, nursed them. He looked at her kindly but in silence. She told him indignantly about how they had grabbed her when she was singing in her head and not looking, and how they had tossed her out of his church. A old heifer like me, she said, straightening up next to Jesus, breathing hard. But he smiled down at her and she felt better instantly and time just seemed to fly by. When they passed her house, forlorn and sagging, weatherbeaten and patched, by the side of the road, she did not even notice it, she was so happy to be out walking along the highway with Jesus.

She broke the silence once more to tell Jesus how glad she was that he had come, how she had often looked at his picture hanging on her wall (she hoped he didn't know she had stolen it) over her bed, and how she had never expected to see him down here in person. Jesus gave her one of his beautiful smiles and they walked on. She did not know where they were going; someplace wonderful, she suspected. The ground was like clouds under their feet, and she felt she could walk forever without becoming the least bit tired. She even began to sing out loud some of the old spirituals she loved, but she didn't want to annoy Jesus, who looked so thoughtful, so she quieted down. They walked on, looking straight over the treetops into the sky, and the smiles that played over her dry wind-cracked face were like first clean ripples across a stagnant pond. On they walked without stopping.

The people in church never knew what happened to the old woman; they never mentioned her to one another or to anybody else. Most of them heard sometime later than an old colored woman fell dead along the highway. Silly as it seemed, it appeared she had walked herself to death. Many of the black families along the road said they had seen the old lady high-stepping down the highway; sometimes jabbering in a low insistent voice, sometimes singing, sometimes merely gesturing excitedly with her hands. Other times silent and smiling, looking at the sky. She had been alone, they said. Some of them wondered aloud where the old woman had been going so stoutly that it had worn her heart out. They guessed maybe she had relatives across the river, some miles away, but none of them really knew.

Alice Walker

 **Do you think Alice Walker addressed this story to black people or white?**

I AM JOAQUÍN

(an excerpt)

. . . Here I stand
          before the Court of Justice
             Guilty
for all the glory of my Raza
          to be sentenced to despair.
Here I stand
      Poor in money
      Arrogant with pride
         Bold with Machismo
         Rich in courage
         and
         Wealthy in spirit and faith.
My knees are caked with mud.
My hands calloused from the hoe.
I have made the Anglo rich
         yet
  Equality is but a word,
    the Treaty of Hidalgo has been broken
  and is but another treacherous promise.
My land is lost
        and stolen,
My culture has been raped,
      I lengthen
      the line at the welfare door
and fill the jails with crime.
      These then
are the rewards
        this society has
For sons of Chiefs
        and Kings
        and bloody Revolutionists.
Who
gave a foreign people
      all their skills and ingenuity

to pave the way with Brains and Blood
for
those hordes of Gold starved
                Strangers
Who
changed our language
and plagiarized our deeds
           as feats of valor
           of their own.
They frowned upon our way of life
  and took what they could use.
         Our Art
         Our Literature
         Our Music, they ignored
so they left the real things of value
and grabbed at their own destruction
           by their Greed and Avarice
They overlooked that cleansing fountain of
           nature and brotherhood
  Which is Joaquin.
        We start to MOVE.
  La Raza!
Mejicano!
  Español!
    Latino!
      Hispano!
        Chicano!
or whatever I call myself,
      I look the same
      I feel the same
      I cry
        and
      Sing the same
I am the masses of my people and
I refuse to be absorbed.
      I am Joaquin
The odds are great
but my spirit is strong
           My faith unbreakable
           My blood is pure
I am Aztec Prince and Christian Christ
      I SHALL ENDURE!
      I WILL ENDURE!

                Rodolfo Gonzales

States' Rights vs. Indian Sovereignty

The position of the Native in American society is unique. By virtue of invasion by foreign peoples, and because the Indian ceded land in payment for which the U.S. Government made certain commitments, the Native American tribes have a relationship directly with the U.S. Government.

Treaties were make with the United States; treaties which are inviolate in the eyes of national and international law. The treaties, commitments, and agreements are with the government on the federal level.

Thus the Indian tribes, with their reservations geographically located within the states, are political and economic entities with their own tribal governments, their own judicial systems, and their own police force.

Within the last few years, however, there has come about what can only be considered a massive attack against the Indian nations, their sovereignty, their right to self-determination, and their special relationship with the federal government. In New Mexico particularly, this power play has increased to an alarming degree.

Recent judicial decisions on Indian water rights have placed the Pueblo Indians "on the same level as all other citizens." This is rank injustice and attacks the very heart of Indian life.

. . .

"States' Rights" is given as the goal of the last several Administrations. That is to say, under the guise of "decentralization" the states are to take over all kinds of functions, including jurisdiction over reservation affairs.

. . .

"Operation Mangle" will be the result of the currently increasing trend on the part of such states as New Mexico to seize control of the Indian reservations, if we allow our vigilance to lag.

Excerpt from an editorial in WASSAJA

Woman is . . .

Feelings, moods, and attitude . . . rule a woman,
*   not facts, reason, nor logic.*

By herself woman is all mixed-up but superb as an auxiliary
*   (Genesis: helper).*

Woman is inanimate or on the defensive
*   until you create a feeling such as praise.*
*   Then she goes all out.*

Never scold or explain when she is angry,
*   remember she is feeling not thinking. . . .*

Stop bossing; just manipulate her in her feelings. . . .

The acquisition of knowledge or responsibilities
*   does not lessen women's need for support,*
*   guidance, and control. Quite the contrary.*

Why ask women when they only need to be told?
*   Why ask women when they hope to be taken?*

G. C. Payetter

You may be growing more like a machine every day, but try to develop yourself so that you will remain a ballbearing mechanism and not a simple abacus. The time will come when she demands the right to step out and become a personality, but if she is worth having she will soon tire of that and reassume her proper role . . . . If she is a gentle little homebody who thinks ninety-nine cents is so much cheaper than a dollar, get down on your knees at night and thank God for the many blessings bestowed upon you . . . You can live most happily with her for a lifetime if you will always remember that she is a different sort of an animal, created specially for a certain purpose, and that the easy companionship that may exist between males is forever impossible between you two.

Joseph Peck

84

LINGUISTIC SEXISM-
A NEO-FEMINIST PERSPECTIVE

The institutions of a society are concretizations of its *Weltanschauung,* or world-view. Neo-feminism, or the current women's liberation movement, is at its most fundamental an analysis and critique of Western culture's *Weltanschauung,* and neo-feminist analysts and critics have been especially concerned with certain institutions which they have considered patriarchal in function and damaging to women. Language is one of the most important of those institutions.

Many neo-feminist articles have appeared on the question of sexism in language. Writers such as Mary Orovan in her work on "humanizing English" and Varda One and Ruth Todasco in their feminist dictionaries have pointed out how the marginal and object status of women is linguistically reflected. And Ethel Strainchamps in "Our Sexist Language" comments on why this fact is crucial in terms of cultural analysis:

Early in this century, anthropologists made a discovery that transformed the nature of their own discipline and of several related ones—linguistics most of all. They found that by painstakingly examining a language they could learn more about the culture of the people who spoke the language than any number of its native speakers, however willing, could tell them.*

Strainchamps goes on to argue that English "retains more vestiges of the archaic sexual attitudes than any other civilized tongue" (241).

But skewed language, neo-feminists assert, not only reveals a culture's bias; it is a form of oppression itself because it in turn skews society's ability to perceive both its own biases and the reality they contradict. Ruth Herschberger, in her classic 1948 study, *Adam's Rib,* showed how language has worked to blind some of our society's supposedly objective scientists to the fact that they were rewriting science along the lines of male-supremacist thinking and myth. Biologists and psychologists have frequently been guilty of structuring linguistically the questions they ask in such a way as to guarantee that their research results will coincide with their biases. Defining aggression as male, for example, has often meant that female research subjects which exhibited aggression were either said to have exhibited some other trait or to be abnormal and "masculine."

Skewed language also oppresses by shaping the self-perceptions of individuals. Neo-feminists have pointed out that English contains many words which are derogatory to women as women and which have no male counterparts; it also has a male-dominant pronoun structure and male-dominant gender signal system. All of these characteristics of the language affect women's self-esteem and self-image.

Among the words that oppress are the infinite variety of those concerning woman's sexuality. Some reduce women to animals—*cold fish, bird*; some to parts of their own bodies—*piece of ass, cunt*; some to inanimate objects—*doll.* The facts that words referring to women—*female, womanish,* and the like are used derogatorily, that when *women* or *women's* is placed before another word, the result is a diminishing—*woman doctor,* and that to feminize a title—*jockey, jockette, suffragette* as opposed to *suffragist*—is to belittle, indicate how English usage reflects and perpetuates a negative attitude

Continued

*Ethel Strainchamps, "Our Sexist Language," in *Woman in Sexist Society: Studies in Power and Powerlessness,* eds. Vivian Gornick and B. K. Moran (New York: Basic Books, 1971), p. 240.

toward women and negative self-images in women. Words such as *chairman, spokesman*, diminish women by indicating linguistically that male dominance is normative, as does the use of *man* for *human being* or *person*. Neo-feminists believe that there is no true generic which is gender-linked; they argue, for example, that if you tell someone a story about "prehistoric man" your listener gets a male image, and if asked to draw an illustration of "prehistoric man," would be much more likely than not to draw a male figure. Also indicative of a male-dominant norm is the linguistic double-standard—*playboy* or *don juan* vs. *loose woman* or *slut*, the glamorous *bachelor* vs. the contemptuous *spinster, master* vs. *mistress*.

There are words that indicate that maleness is dependent upon dominance and true femaleness implies a properly deferential attitude to males: consider that the *bitch*, a woman who is not submissive and deferential, *castrates* her man. There are words which indicate that importance and maleness are conjoined: consider the irony of calling Kate Millett's book *Sexual Politics* a *seminal* work. There are the titles *Miss* and *Mrs.* which distinguish women by marital status as men are not distinguished, identifying women by their relationship to a man and permitting their sexual availability to be assessed. There is a whole vocabulary of woman-hating, although there is no comparable vocabulary of misandry, or man-hating. A *bastard* or *son-of-a-bitch* is a man whose *mother* is to be despised. A *whore* has *customers*, not brothers in sin/crime.

And there is the so-called generic use of the male singular pronoun. The pronoun structure of the English language can literally make women linguistically invisible.

Consider the grammatically impeccable statement attributed to one male sympathizer with abortion law repeal: "Everyone should be able to decide for himself whether or not to have an abortion."

The recent work of neo-feminist linguists such as Robin Lakoff of

---

It is time for women to ask some basic questions

 **Briefly answer the three questions asked here. Then weave your answers into a short story that presents your position.**

Can women change their own image —or are the media going to do it for them?

Is it possible to have advertising that does not exploit —or is that a contradiction of terms?

Is liberation going to be sold as a product with planned obsolescence?

These are the questions we all have to face. The answers will be varied, depending upon the politics or positions of the women making change.

It is our own feeling that the *selling* of an image, no matter how liberated, is the wrong approach. Co-optation through consumption may prove to be the greatest threat to the women's movement.

Judith Miller and Leah D. Margulies

the University of California at Berkeley shows how women's self-esteem and perceptions of their own power and importance are lower than man's, and how this fact is perpetuated linguistically and reflected in women's more frequent use of certain apologetic or self-effacing syntactic modes. For example, women more commonly than men use tag questions (A is B, *isn't it?*) rather than flat statements (A is B) and request (*Would you* please shut the door?) rather than commands (Please shut the door).

Neo-feminists, believing that sexism in language skews women's self-perceptions and their image in the minds of both women and men, and helps to reinforce the sexism in our culture, try to avoid the kinds of usages which belittle women. They tend, for example, to avoid mentioning women second, deprecating their sexuality, or referring to them as a group in diminishing or contemptuous terms. They do not set women off by their sex linguistically from the standard, as in *lady doctor*, because such a usage conveys the idea that there is a central type of humanity and women do not qualify for membership in it. They do not refer to women as members of a subspecies, such as *the fair sex*, because a subspecies is again different from the human standard, and such usages frustrate women's image of themselves as, first of all, human persons. They avoid the kinds of words, word order, and gender signals which are male-

dominant or which separate femaleness linguistically from humanness.

Neo-feminists are dealing with the power of language to demean women also by creating or emphasizing words and phrases such as *conditioning, Manglish, the feminine mystique*, etc., to help women understand how they have been taught to feel inferior and secondary, and how to protest. They are trying to provide a new unskewed vocabulary and to develop a linguistic mode which conditions positively, describing female sexuality and femaleness itself in complementary terms. Such expressions as *taking back our heads* and *herstory* (for history) signal neo-feminist defiance of the force of sexual conditioning and determination to reverse its effects. Among the linguistic devices neo-feminists have developed for undercutting sexual myths and stereotypes and for anatomizing sexism are phrases such as *the myth of women's inferiority* and *the myth of the vaginal orgasm*. Neo-feminists counter the stereotypes which have been used to cast aspersions and disapproval on rebellious and unsubmissive women—*bitch, castrating women*—by substituting sympathetic terms like *sister* which suggest solidarity among rebellious women and a positive attitude toward them. They point to how roles and role behavior are culturally sanctioned and taught to both sexes rather than inherent in phrases like *sex-role conditioning*, and how personal characteristics

are assigned to members of one sex or the other without regard for individual disposition in phrases like *sex-role stereotype.*

A development of primary importance, as has become obvious in the literature and press coverage of the women's liberation movement, is the invention of words to describe the neo-feminist political outlook and share this outlook with people previously unable to articulate their perceptions of sexual inequality. To describe the relations between the sexes as power-structured and discriminatory, we have *male chauvinism, male supremacy, sexism, sexual politics.* To relate women's problems to those of people in other oppressed groups, neo-feminists have been using terms such as *colonization* and *psychology of oppression.* To protest individuals' acts of misogyny they have produced the terms *male chauvinist (pig), male supremacist, sexist, Aunt Tom.*

It bears repeating that women's language has traditionally differed from men's in that it has lacked expressions of sexual hatred and degradation of the opposite sex. It has been perhaps too deficient in expressions of anger. This is not to say that women have not to some extent used the same language of anger as men, but as neo-feminists are pointing out, this language is in many cases alien to women; it cannot serve the same expletive function for them as it does for male users because it is misogynistic.

Continued

When a woman calls someone a *bastard*, for example, she is speaking from within a male framework in which the legitimacy of women's sexual behavior, unlike men's, depends upon their legal connections to a member of the opposite sex. Neo-feminists would tend to substitute a term like *male chauvinist* for one like *bastard* when possible in order to express anger without colluding with sexism.

In attempting linguistically to affirm femaleness, neo-feminists make much use of words linked to the concepts of androgyny, personhood, and selfhood, and tend to reject expressions denoting a separate "nature" for women, as do words linked to the concept of "femininity." Neo-feminists use terms such as *shuffling* and *gestures of submission* to expose the contradiction between "femininity" (an attitude of deference toward males) and humanity or personhood.

Looking at the overall picture of neo-feminist writing, one can see, in addition to reforms in language, the beginnings of a new style. As many neo-feminists have noted, the linguistic mode characteristic of our male-dominant and hierarchical culture is the authoritative and declarative. Because they reject authoritarianism as oppressive to all people and base their politics on personal experience, neo-feminists tend to reject using statements to communicate what are often essentially only opinions, and their style sometimes then seems to be more descriptive than declarative; it is more inclined to the many-faceted, less structured by the desire to assert one idea to the exclusion of others than to convey the multiple and personal character of experience. This is not to say that neo-feminist writers are unable to speak with authority about their experiences. It is simply to say that they affirm, in style and in language, the idea that each

individual has a unique potential and vision and set of perceptions which embody the integrity of that human being, be s/he female or male.

Ellen Morgan

List at least five examples of sexism in the English language. If you know a foreign language, list instances of sexism in it also.

Write down what you think is the main idea expressed in this essay. Now think of that idea in terms of the propaganda in various media. Write an essay in which you defend the idea or attack it, or simply weave together what you consider to be some points in favor and against.

It is women who set the stage and largely control the players in important sections of American life. America is a woman's world, a world in which, as a Chinese woman, Helena Kuo, remarked, women have succeeded in everything except the art of being truly feminine.

Eric John Dingwall

Playboy fills a special need...

For the insecure young man with newly acquired time and money on his hands who still feels uncertain about his consumer skills, *Playboy* supplies a comprehensive and authoritative guidebook to this foreboding new world to which he now has access. It tells him not only who to be; it tells him *how* to be it, and even provides consolation outlets for those who secretly feel they have not quite made it.

In supplying for the other-directed consumer of leisure both the normative identity image and the means for achieving it, *Playboy* relies on a careful integration of copy and advertising material. The comic book that appeals to a younger generation with an analogous problem skillfully intersperses illustrations of incredibly muscled men and excessively mammalian women with advertisements for body-building gimmicks and foam rubber brassiere supplements. Thus the thin-chested comic book readers of both sexes are thoughtfully supplied with both the ends and the means for attaining a spurious brand of maturity. *Playboy* merely continues the comic book tactic for the next age group. Since within every identity crisis, whether in 'teens or twenties, there is usually a sexual identity problem, *Playboy* speaks to those who desperately want to know what it means to be a *man*, and more specifically a *male*, in today's world.

Both the image of man and the means for its attainment exhibit a remarkable consistency in *Playboy*. The skilled consumer is cool and unruffled. He savors sports cars, liquor, high fidelity and book club selections with a casual, unhurried aplomb. Though he must certainly *have* and *use* the latest consumption item, he must not permit himself to get too attached to it. The style will change and he must always be ready to adjust. His persistent anxiety that he may mix a drink incorrectly, enjoy a jazz group that is passé, or wear last year's necktie style is comforted by an authoritative tone in *Playboy* beside which papal encyclicals sound irresolute.

"Don't hesitate," he is told, "this assertive, self-assured weskit is what every man of taste wants for the fall season." Lingering doubts about his masculinity are extirpated by the firm assurance that "real men demand this ruggedly masculine smoke" (cigar ad). Though "the ladies will swoon for you, no matter what they promise, don't give them a puff. This cigar is for men only." A fur-lined canvas field jacket is described as "the most masculine thing since the cave man." What to be and how to be it are both made unambiguously clear.

But since being a male necessitates some kind of relationship to females, *Playboy* fearlessly confronts this problem too, and solves it by the consistent application of the same formula. Sex becomes one of the items of leisure activity that the knowledgeable consumer of leisure handles with his characteristic skill and detachment. The girl becomes a desirable, indeed an indispensable "Playboy accessory."

In a question-answering column entitled: "The Playboy Advisor," queries about smoking equipment (how to break in a meerschaum pipe), cocktail preparation (how to mix a "Yellow Fever") and whether or not to wear suspenders with a vest, alternate with questions about what to do with girls who complicate the cardinal principle of casualness, either by suggesting marriage or by some other impulsive gesture toward permanent relationship. The infallible answer from the oracle never varies: sex must be contained, at all costs, within the entertainment-recreation area. Don't let her get "serious."

After all, the most famous feature of the magazine is its monthly fold-out photo of a *play*mate. She is the symbol par excellence of recreational sex. When play time is over, the playmate's function ceases, so she must be made to understand the rules of the game. As the crew-cut young man in a *Playboy* cartoon says to the rumpled and disarrayed girl he is passionately embracing, "Why speak of love at a time like this?"

Harvey Cox

Woman defined . . .

Women have discovered that the English language functions as a heavy whip-welding master to keep women in their place. A sexually expressive girl feels the epithetic whip early on. Chit, minx, slut, and now more ambiguously, chick. A slut is "a bold or impudent girl: humorous usage." The epithet whips hard, intended to disturb and control feeling. "A woman who is careless of her appearance," "a woman of loose character"—"slut" still generates fear and self-contempt, shaping a girl to fit the traditional slots patriarchy has created for her sexual status: whore, wife, old maid.

We are aware that English language dictionaries do not distinguish between girl and woman, and that terms designating girl and woman mean prostitute. A "working girl" is "a woman who works" and is U.S. slang for prostitute. A "girl" is 1. a female of any age, single or married 2. a female servant: maid 3. a female employee (as a secretary) 4. prostitute 5. sweetheart 6. daughter. No matter how developed in years and experience a woman is, she is supposed to believe it is a compliment to be called a girl. This epithet is a masterstroke. It implies that women never develop. Their life experiences are not affirmed. How can the experience of women be taken seriously, except first by women themselves. Patriarchy is more interested in the experience of dolphins.

We have discovered that words meaning whore apply to any woman, single or married, employed or unemployed, high, low, or middle class, who offends or appeals sexually to male sensibilities. A lady who makes men uncomfortable about themselves is no longer a lady, as by definition a lady is a woman bred to please. Both a lady and a whore are supposed to give men what they think they want in the way they want it. A woman is put into one category or the other depending on the male's perception of his own need and comfort. For that reason, a woman testifying to rape is automatically regarded by men as whore, as having asked for what she gets. Their presumption that man is the natural

---

It is written. A daughter is a vain treasure to her father. From anxiety about her he does not sleep at night; during her early years lest she be seduced, in her adolescence lest she go astray, in her marriageable years lest she does not find a husband, when she is married lest she be childless, and when she is old lest she practice witchcraft.
Talmud *(Ben Sira. Sanhedrin 100 b)*

---

protector of women makes it painful if not impossible for them to admit that women are victims of deliberate male violence.

Language reflects the self-deluding myths of patriarchal man. However brutalized man is, women are brought up to look to him positively as "protector" and "provider." The language itself—man-protector-provider—has a positive appeal which is intended to obscure its real effect. These male roles enforce woman's dependency and have traditionally allowed for the male's crippling control of her sexual experience and self-image.

In any circumstances, a woman whose sexuality is apparent is considered implicitly whorish, unless she proves she is a lady. Then her status may be turned against her with epithets such as prudish, old-fashioned, frigid, unresponsive, uninteresting. Somehow the "sexy lady" has become a cultural ideal, celebrated just about everywhere, in film, music, advertising. From the male point of view, there is no problem involved in being a whorish lady that glamour and masculine attention can't solve. But from a woman's experience of it, the sexy lady ideal is ideally exhausting. A wondrous mechanism for the castration of women.

Class consciousness created by patriarchal institutions gives an illusion of dignity to the woman who regards herself as a lady. She pays for the illusion by denying her sexuality. Every woman has heard the intonation of contempt in the word "lady." It is often used as a generalized term of abuse. The terrible irony is that women are still conditioned to believe that "ladylike" behavior guarantees respect.

A woman's appearance, behavior, language, gestures, manners from the most natural to the most artificial, and her achievements, leave her vulnerable to self-damaging epithets. There is no sanctuary for a woman in patriarchal society, because womanness itself is deprecated.

Ruth Todasco

Join a group of your classmates and together make as long a list as possible of the terms used to describe women. Include slang, vulgar, standard, formal, and legal terms.

Divide the list among you so that each person has approximately the same number of terms. Look up the words in suitable dictionaries, and list all the definitions given.

Compile all the words and definitions; study and discuss them carefully.

Write an essay on the image of women in the English language, using the words and the dictionary definitions to support and illustrate your thesis.

Using the same criteria, write another essay that explores the image of men as they are reflected in the English language.

What insights about the famale and the male have you gained?

To what extent has the language influenced your thinking and attitudes?

In which areas have you been influenced with subtle propaganda?

Gather a group of friends of both sexes and try the communication technique recommended by Marge Piercy. Write about the experience in a short essay.

COUNCILS

We must sit down
and reason together.
We must sit down:
men standing want to hold forth.
They rain down upon faces lifted.
We must sit down on the floor
on the earth
on stones and mats and blankets.
There must be no front to the speaking
no platform, no rostrum,
no stage or table.
We will not crane
to see who is speaking.
Perhaps we should sit in the dark.
In the dark we could utter our feelings.
In the dark we could propose
and describe and suggest.
In the dark we could not see who speaks
and only the words
would say what they say.
No one would speak more than twice.
No one would speak less than once.
Thus saying what we feel and what we want,
what we fear for ourselves and each other
into the dark, perhaps we could begin
to begin to listen.
Perhaps we should talk in groups
the size of new families,
not more, never more than twenty.
Perhaps we should start by speaking softly.

The women must learn to dare to speak.
The men must learn to bother to listen.
The women must learn to say I think this is so.
The men must learn to stop dancing solos on the ceiling.
After each speaks, she or he
will say a ritual phrase:
It is not I who speaks but the wind.
Wind blows through me.
Long after me, is the wind.

Marge Piercy

LEARNING TO BE A PRINCESS

. . . A close examination of the treatment of women in fairy tales reveals certain patterns which are keenly interesting not only in themselves, but also as material which has undoubtedly played a major contribution in forming the sexual role concept of children, and in suggesting to them the limitations that are imposed by sex upon a person's changes of success in various endeavors. It is now being questioned whether those traits that have been characterized as feminine have a biological or a cultural basis: discarding the assumptions of the past, we are asking what is inherent in our nature, and what has become ours through the gentle but forcible process of acculturation.

. . . Millions of women must surely have formed their psycho-sexual self-concepts, and their ideas of what sort of behavior would be rewarded, and of the nature of reward itself, in part from their favorite fairy tales. These stories have been made the repositories of the dreams, hopes, and fantasies of generations of girls. . . .

Certain premises and patterns emerge at once, of which only the stereotyped figure of the wicked step-mother has received much general notice. The beauty contest is a constant and primary device in many of the stories. Where there are several daughters in a family, or several unrelated girls in a story, the prettiest is invariably singled out and designated for reward, or first for punishment and later for reward. Beautiful girls are never ignored; they may be oppressed at first by wicked figures, as the jealous Queen persecutes Snow White, but ultimately they are chosen for reward.

. . . Good-temper and meekness are so regularly associated with beauty, and ill-temper with ugliness, that this in itself must influence children's expectations. The most famous example of this associational pattern occurs in ''Cinderella,'' with the opposition of the ugly, cruel, bad-

Briefly summarize a fairy tale that you especially liked when you were a child.

Write an essay describing the attitudes it projects toward the roles of the sexes, and discussing the extent to which you agree with those attitudes today.

Then, on the basis of the exploration in your essay, give a two-minute speech either defending or refuting Lieberman's position.

Write the script for a TV puppet show for children. In it, avoid all the patterns described by Lieberman. Check both adults' and children's reactions to it.

tempered older sisters to the younger, beautiful, sweet Cinderella, but in *The Blue Fairy Book* it also occurs in many other stories, such as ''Beauty and the Beast'' and ''Toads and Diamonds.''

. . . The stories reflect an intensely competitive spirit: they are frequently about contests, for which there can be only one winner because there is only one prize. Girls win the prize if they are bold, active, and lucky. If a child identifies with the beauty, she may learn to be suspicious of ugly girls, who are portrayed as cruel, sly, and unscrupulous in these stories; if she identifies with the plain girls, she may learn to be suspicious and jealous of pretty girls, beauty being a gift of fate, not something that can be attained. There are no examples of a crossed-pattern, that is, of plain but good-tempered girls. It is a psychological truth that as children, and as women, girls fear homeliness (even attractive girls are frequently convinced that they are plain), and this fear is a major source of anxiety, diffidence, and convictions of inadequacy and inferiority among women. It is probably also a source of envy and discord among them. Girls may be predisposed to imagine that there is a link between the lovable face and the lovable character, and to fear, if plain themselves, that they will also prove to be unpleasant, thus using the patterns to set up self-fulfilling prophecies.

Marcia Lieberman

The Hand That Rocked the Cradle Points the Way

Read the following excerpt and decide what appeals this passage makes? Mark the passages that are persuasive. What makes them so?

Using a different code, mark the passages where the persuasion is unsuccessful. Why do they fail? Rewrite them, presenting the same argument so that you feel they are more convincing.

Read your version to the class so that other students can evaluate your argument.

Women seek the humanization of the culture.

This is a very large demand. Its achievement might almost be called a miracle.

Well, humans who can produce new humans are not intimidated by miracles. So we're working on the problem.

I suggest that women have found the way to achieve it. And the secret is so simple, it's not surprising that it has been overlooked.

Women have learned that, as the Beatles told us a while ago, we can get by "with a little help from our friends." This idea of helping one another, of working cooperatively, is, I believe, the key to the whole thing. And it is an area in which the new woman is pointing the way.

The most remarkable idea to come from the women's movement is that of sisterhood. This is not a new idea—the concept of the common humanness of all peoples has been articulated throughout history. Each year, on Brotherhood Day, it's trotted out so that everyone can remember that it's still around. Everyone can remember how long it's been since he last remembered it. But, of course, no one takes it seriously, or intends to live by it.

George Bernard Shaw made this very clear in a brief exchange in his play "Candida," written 80 years ago. In a conversation between the Reverend James Morell and his secretary, she refers to a group as "half a dozen ignorant and conceited costermongers without five shillings between them." He replies, "Ah, but you see, they're near relatives of mine." When she expresses surprise at this, he explains, "We have the same Father in heaven." Shaw's stage direction is that her response is given in a relieved tone; she says, "Oh, is that all?"

Of course, no one ever seriously expected to live by this philosophy.

But within the past few years, we have seen women take this old idea and infuse new life into it. They have made it workable, and in many, many instances they have made it work.

You know, the principal characteristic of the life of modern woman has been her isolation. The older image of women leaning across the back fence to talk to one another has been replaced by the more up-to-date one of the woman alone in her house talking to her friend by telephone. Reaching out for some human contact.

Women were isolated at home, with a household which didn't need that much cleaning, and children who had their own absolutely inviolate schedule to maintain. The mother's schedule was to meet all needs and requirements of every member of the family except herself. She got up when the children had to go to school, went out when they had to be driven to Little League, or piano lessons, or the orthodontist, stayed home when they were ill, prepared dinner so it would be ready when her husband came home, and went to bed when he needed to rest so that he would be ready for another day at the office. In short, she lived a model nineteenth-century life, while her husband participated in the twentieth century, and her children prepared for the twenty-first. She made few friends of her own, and had only a very restricted relationship with those women she did know.

Continued

Did anyone ever stop to think why it was that women gathered together to talk to one another at parties? They were treated with scorn because they chose those opportunities to compare notes about their households and their children. Why didn't anyone realize that parties offered women the only opportunity they had for shop talk? All men engage in shop talk. Women also need an opportunity to talk about their work.

Another thing that kept women isolated was that confounded pedestal we are always hearing about. Try standing on a pedestal for an hour or two and see how lonely you feel up there.

Or, we can take a look at the working woman. She was sentenced to function in what Caroline Bird calls a female "job ghetto." A typist in a typing pool. A saleswoman in a department store. A nurse in a hospital. An elementary school teacher. A worker in a sexually segregated division of a factory. In every instance, the women worked in jobs which were lower paid and offered little or no chance for advancement or additional training. And they always had bosses, managers, principals, or administrators who were men. Above all, the work was not cooperative, interacting work. The women worked side by side, but each one was alone, doing her job on her own.

Women's opinions and women's attitudes were consistently denigrated. "Just like a woman," the world said. "What can you expect of a woman?" Women's expressions of feelings were called whining, bitching, castrating, and nagging. They were really downright unfeminine!

Every woman was taught to consider every other woman a competitor. When the only goal was to get a man, sometimes any man, every other woman became a rival in that effort. If a woman had a man, the other women continued to be rivals—someone might get him away. And when he's all you have for financial security, for social status, and for a legal position, he's very important.

If you had a job, you were competing with every other woman who held the identical job for those very few, very slight advancements that might be made.

Into this dreary picture came the idea of sisterhood. And the world was turned upside down. It was positively exhilarating for women to realize that they could actually talk to other women and could depend upon other women listening to them seriously.

When half the world recognizes one another as sisters, it doesn't take very long before they look at the other half and recognize them as brothers. It is exciting even to think about the improvements we can make in the world when we truly recognize our common humanity.

What Shaw saw—80 years ago

Now of all the idealist abominations that make society pestiferous, I doubt if there be any so mean as that of forcing self-sacrifice on a woman under pretence that she likes it; and, if she ventures to contradict the pretence, declaring her no true woman.

• • •

The domestic career is no more natural to all women than the military career is natural to all men; and although in a population emergency it might become necessary for every ablebodied woman to risk her life in childbed just as it might become necessary in a military emergency for every man to risk his life in the battlefield, yet even then it would by no means follow that the child-bearing would endow the mother with domestic aptitudes and capacities as it would endow her with milk.

• • •

A whole basketful of ideals of the most sacred quality will be smashed by the achievement of equality for women and men. Those who shrink from such a clatter and breakage may comfort themselves with the reflection that the replacement of the broken goods will be prompt and certain. It is always a case of "The ideal is dead: long live the ideal!" And the advantage of the work of destruction is that every new ideal is less of an illusion than the one it has supplanted; so that the destroyer of ideals, though denounced as an enemy of society, is in fact sweeping the world clear of lies.

Why do these statements sound contemporary?

A Fable of Fallacies II

Proper Gander and Mother Goose were having a family argument.

"Why can't you spend more time with me and the goslings?" she demanded. "All you do is strut around the farmyard thrusting your opinions on creatures that don't want them. Why, only yesterday Flora Fowl was saying to a group of old hens that she thought you were the biggest bore on the farm. I heard it only by accident and it made me blush for shame."

"They're stereotyping me," complained Proper Gander, "just because they think they've found something nasty to gossip about. Those old hens are all the same. They're never happy unless they're running somebody down. I'm just an ordinary, quiet fellow who goes about minding his own business like every other member of the farm community."

"That kind of plain-folks talk doesn't impress me," said Mother Goose. "I know you for what you are, so don't try to talk your way out of it. Nothing gives you more pleasure than airing your opinions."

"That's not true," objected Proper Gander in a hurt tone.

"Scores of ducks, hens, and even turkeys tell me daily how knowledgeable and wise I am. Why can't you believe what they do? They can't all be wrong."

"There you go again with your usual bandwagon tactics, trying to impress me with phony numbers. The fact of the matter is that you've got only one friend who'll say a good word for you and that's that decrepit and stupid old Mallard Drake who, for some reason I've never been able to understand, thinks you are beyond reproach."

"You're distorting the truth," replied Proper Gander. "Old Mallard Drake may have lived a long time, but he's a fine, wise old bird."

"Well, you won't find me wasting any euphemisms on him. I think he's a lazy, corn-stealing no-good. If you had any sense of dignity and responsibility, you'd show how much you love me and your family by spending more time with us instead of going all over the place with him. At least you could take the goslings swimming sometimes. Why should I shoulder the entire responsibility for looking after them? I want to be free to do my own thing once in a while."

"That's never been the custom with geese. Mother geese have always taken care of the goslings so that the ganders were free to roam the farm and do other important things. It's unthinkable that I should have to contend with domestic duties."

"Well, times have changed. Females have equal rights with males, even in the farmyard, or are you so out of date you haven't heard? Now the goslings are down by the pond. I must get ready to go to a hen party. I have to rehearse my speech."

Proper Gander arched his neck defiantly, but, slowly, he waddled off toward the duck pond.

"Females have equal rights with males!" he muttered. "What is the world coming to?"

Where did we come from?

part

2

ropaganda of the Past

"GIVE ME LIBERTY, OR GIVE ME DEATH!"

PATRICK HENRY delivering his great speech on the Rights of the Colonies, before the Virginia Assembly, convened at Richmond March 23rd 1775. Concluding with the above sentiment, which became the war cry of the Revolution.

Propaganda has roots deep in history. No matter how far back we look into recorded time, we are reminded of its impact. People living in ancient societies were persuaded to believe in one thing or another by leaders, priests, and others.

From its beginnings, the Roman Catholic Church has aggressively used missionaries to persuade pagan peoples to turn to Christianity. (The term "propaganda" came into the English language from *congregatio de propaganda fide*—the congregation for propagating the faith—which was the name of a committee of Roman Catholic cardinals in charge of foreign missions.)

The earliest known Christian influence in the English-speaking world occurred when the Romans conquered Britain, in the first century. From that time on, Roman Catholicism was carried all over Roman-occupied Britain. The process of Christianization suffered a temporary setback during the pagan Anglo-Saxon invasions of the British Isles during the fifth century. However, missionaries from Ireland and Wales, together with some aid from St. Augustine, revived Christianity once more and spread it throughout Britain.

By medieval times, Britain was a Roman Catholic country. The faithful erected lovely churches in the rural areas and magnificent cathedrals in the cities as testaments to the work of God. The congregations that flocked to them and sat on the floor in the naves were largely illiterate. Since the people could not read, biblical scenes were painted on

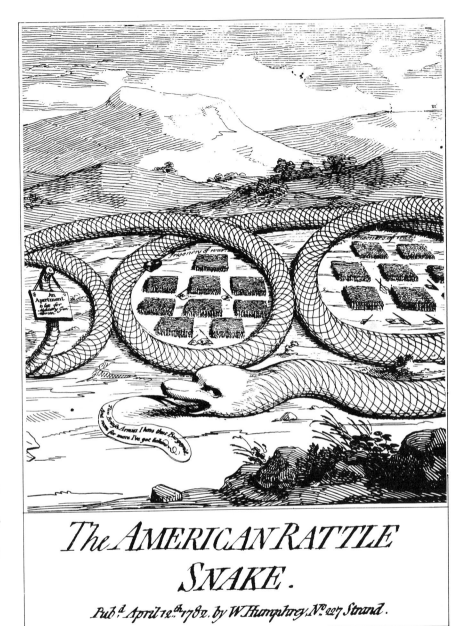

The AMERICAN RATTLE SNAKE.

Pub.d April 12.th 1782. by W.Humphrey N.o 227 Strand.

the walls, and religious symbols were contained in the beautiful art of the stained-glass windows. At the altar, simple miracle plays were enacted for the congregations. In this way, they received the Holy message.

During the reign of Henry VIII, England broke away from the established influence of Rome and disavowed the Pope. Roman Catholic Englishmen were persuaded, verbally or physically, that they should join the Protestant Church of England or suffer horrible penalties. During this era, and at later times, there was counter-Catholic propaganda. The biblical messages on walls were white-

The BLOODY MASSACRE perpetrated in King Street BOSTON on March 5th 1770 by a party of the 29th REGT

BUTCHER'S HALL

Engrav'd Printed & Sold by Paul Revere Boston

Unhappy BOSTON! see thy Sons deplore,
Thy hallow'd Walks besmear'd with guiltless Gore.
While faithless P—n and his savage Bands.
With murd'rous Rancour stretch their bloody Hands;
Like fierce Barbarians grinning o'er their Prey.
Approve the Carnage, and enjoy the Day.

If scalding drops from Rage from Anguish Wrung
If speechless Sorrows lab'ring for a Tongue
Or if a weeping World can ought appease
The plaintive Ghosts of Victims such as these:
The Patriot's copious Tears for each are shed.
A glorious Tribute which embalms the Dead

But know FATE summons to that awful Goal.
Where JUSTICE strips the Murd'rer of his Soul:
Should venal C—ts the scandal of the Land.
Snatch the relentless Villain from her Hand.
Keen Execrations on this Plate inscrib'd.
Shall reach a JUDGE who never can be brib'd.

The unhappy Sufferers were Messrs SAML GRAY SAML MAVERICK, JAMS CALDWELL, CRISPUS ATTUCKS & PATK CARR

Killed. Six wounded; two of them (CHRISTR MONK & JOHN CLARK) Mortally

Published in 1770 by Paul Revere Boston

washed, stained-glass windows were smashed, and ornate Roman Catholic carvings and icons were removed, destroyed, or mutilated. The orders of monks and friars were suppressed, and Henry VIII sold great parts of the confiscated abbey lands to peers, public servants, and merchants.

Out of the Church of England grew the Puritan movement. Puritans were a Protestant sect who were dissatisfied with what they considered the popish trappings of the Church of England. They created their own severe kind of religious society. The Puritan movement, however, ran into opposition from many circles. Attempts were made to discriminate against, and even suppress, them. Eventually, a small Puritan group decided to seek religious and commercial freedom in the New World. These Puritans were the founders of the first American colonies. Soon they advertised in Europe for more settlers to join them, but, as the colonies grew in population and became established, they discovered that they were unavoidably tied commercially and politically to Britain. Because they sought their own commercial freedom, they resented British taxation demands, and other British mercantile considerations. This resentment fomented anger and dissension in America. Before long, it became clear to some Americans that separation from England was the only solution. It was a difficult time. People in England and in America were undecided at first whether the revolutionary tack was the right one to take, or whether right lay with continuing allegiance to England. At first the controversy remained

verbal. Then events led to military confrontation, and the two English-speaking peoples found themselves at war.

Before and after open hostilities, there was a propaganda exchange of proportions never before reached in a human conflict within the English-speaking world.

Today, Americans are looking back and reflecting with interest upon the message and spirit of those times.

TO all Gentlemen VOLUNTEERS, who prefer LIBERTY to SLAVERY, and are hearty Friends to the GRAND *AMERICAN* CAUSE; who are free and willing to serve this STATE, in the Character of a Gentleman MATROSS, and learn the noble Art of Gunnery, in the Massachusetts State Train of Artillery, commanded by Col. THOMAS CRAFTS, now stationed in the Town and Harbour of *BOSTON*, and not to be removed but by Order of the honorable House of Representatives, or Council of said State; let them appear at the Drum-Head, or at the ▬▬▬ where ▬▬▬ shall enter into present Pay ▬▬▬ ▬▬▬ Shillings per Month. For their Encouragement they shall receive *Twenty Dollars* Bounty on passing Muster, one Suit of Regimental Cloathes yearly, a Blanket, &c. with Arms and Accoutrements suitable for a Gentleman Matross. For their further Encouragement, the Colonel would inform all Gentlemen Volunteers, that there are *twenty-two Non-commission Officers in each Company, who receive from three Pounds four and six Pence, to three Pounds twelve per Month*; and as none will be accepted in said Regiment, but Men of good Characters, such only will be promoted, whose steady Conduct and good Behaviour merits it.

☞ *You are desired to take Notice of the difference of Pay and Station.*

A SOCIETY of PATRIOTIC LADIES.

The propaganda literature of the American Revolution is outstanding for its quality. Before the revolution the circular letters of the patriot Samuel Adams and such pamphlets as *Letters from a Pennsylvania Farmer* by John Dickinson sought to inform and unify American opinion in the quarrel with Great Britain. The Declaration of Independence, written by Thomas Jefferson, was a masterpiece of rational propaganda intended to crystallize public opinion at home and justify the controversial American cause abroad. In the darkest days of Valley Forge the radical writer Thomas Paine founded the periodical *The Crisis,* which rallied and sustained American morale for the long struggle. After the war, when controversy raged around the adoption of the Federal Constitution, the articles written by Alexander Hamilton, James Madison, and John Jay, and known collectively as the *Federalist Papers,* explained the new constitution and persuaded Americans to ratify it. A classic of political literature, the *Federalist Papers* was also an effective instrument of propaganda.

Funk & Wagnalls
Standard Reference Encyclopedia

Selling a Revolution

Because humans have always used many kinds of propaganda, we have innumerable examples in our history. Since we cannot study them all, it's useful to focus on a single period to learn how our forebears persuaded one another to take action, or accept a philosophical position, or join a cause.

Among the best propagandists the world has known were the dedicated people who first convinced the American people to support the idea of independence from England, even at the cost of war. Then they persuaded a "candid world" to assist them or, at least, to remain neutral. Finally, they won acceptance of a revolutionary Constitution. All this was accomplished in a relatively short time, and with only limited means of communication.

Here are some of their writings. As you read them, note which persuasive techniques are used. Would they be effective today?

THE HORSE AMERICA, *throwing his Master.*

Pub.d as the Act directs. Aug.st 1.st 1779. by Wm White, Angel Court, Westminster.

Publishing with "utmost freedom" . . .

Be not intimidated, therefore, by any terrors, from publishing with the utmost freedom whatever can be warranted by the laws of your country; nor suffer yourselves to be wheedled out of your liberty by any pretenses of politeness, delicacy, or decency. These, as they are often used, are but three different names for hypocrisy, chicanery, and cowardice. Much less, I presume, will you be discouraged by any pretenses that malignants on this side the water will represent your paper as factious and seditious, or that the great on the other side the water will take offense at them. This dread of representation has had for a long time, in this province, effects very similar to what the physicians call a hydropho or dread of water. It has made us delirious; and we have rushed headlong into the water, till we are almost drowned, out of simple or phrensical fear of it. Believe me, the character of this country has suffered more in Britain by the pusillanimity with which we have borne many insults and indignities from the creatures of power at home and the creatures of those creatures here than it ever did or ever will by the freedom and spirit that has been or will be discovered in writing or action. Believe me, my countrymen, they have imbibed an opinion on the other side the water that we are an ignorant, a timid, and a stupid people; nay, their tools on this side have often the impudence to dispute your bravery. But I hope in God the time is near at hand when they will be fully convinced of your understanding, integrity, and courage.

John Adams, 1765

The American Rattlesnake presenting Monsieur his Ally a Dish of Frogs.

Pub.d by J Barrow. Nov.r 8. 1782. N.o 84 Dorset Street, Salisbury Court, Fleet Street.

Prospect of the Future Glory of America

Fair Freedom now her ensigns bright displays,
And peace and plenty bless the golden days.

. . .

"The patriot's voice shall Eloquence inspire
With Roman splendor and Athenian fire,
At freedom's call, teach manly breasts to glow,
And prompt the tender tear o'er guiltless woe."

John Trumbull, 1770

THE CURIOUS ZEBRA.

London, Printed for G. Johnson as the Act directs 3 Sep.r 1778, and Sold at all the Printshops in London & Westminster.

A Declaration by the Representatives of the UNITED STATES OF AMERICA, in General Congress assembled.

When in the course of human events it becomes necessary for one people to dissolve the political bands which have connected them with another, and to assume among the powers of the earth the separate and equal station to which the laws of nature & of nature's god entitle them, a decent respect to the opinions of mankind requires that they should declare the causes which impel them to the separation.

We hold these truths to be self-evident, that all men are created equal, that they are endowed by their creator with inherent & inalienable rights; that among these are life, & liberty, & the pursuit of happiness; that to secure these rights, governments are instituted among men, deriving their just powers from the consent of the governed; that whenever any form of government becomes destructive of these ends, it is the right of the people to alter or to abolish it, & to institute new government, laying it's foundation on such principles & organising it's powers in such form, as to them shall seem most likely to effect their safety & happiness. prudence indeed will dictate that governments long established should not be changed for light & transient causes: and accordingly all experience hath shewn that mankind are more disposed to suffer while evils are sufferable, than to right themselves by abolishing the forms to which they are accustomed. but when a long train of abuses & usurpations [begun at a distinguished period, &] pursuing invariably the same object, evinces a design to reduce them under absolute Despotism, it is their right, it is their duty, to throw off such government & to provide new guards for their future security. such has been the patient sufferance of these colonies; & such is now the necessity which constrains them to expunge their former systems of government. the history of the present king of Great Britain is a history of unremitting injuries and usurpations, among which appears no solitary fact to contradict the uniform tenor of the rest but all have in direct object the establishment of an absolute tyranny over these states. to prove this, let facts be submitted to a candid world, [for the truth of which we pledge a faith yet unsullied by falsehood]

Dr. Franklin's handwriting

Mr. Adams' hand writing

The argumentative Declaration . . .

 Choose a contemporary issue which is of concern to you. Write a close sentence-by-sentence imitation of the opening two paragraphs of the Declaration of Independence in arguing for your issue.

The Declaration of Independence—1776

In Congress, July 4, 1776

The Unanimous Declaration of The Thirteen United States of America

When in the Course of human events, it becomes necessary for one people to dissolve the political bands which have connected them with another, and to assume among the Powers of the earth, the separate and equal station to which the Laws of Nature and of Nature's God entitle them, a decent respect to the opinions of mankind requires that they should declare the causes which impel them to the separation.

We hold these truths to be self-evident, that all men are created equal, that they are endowed by their Creator with certain unalienable Rights, that among these are Life, Liberty, and the pursuit of Happiness.—That to secure these rights, Governments are instituted among Men, deriving their just powers from the consent of the governed.—That whenever any Form of Government becomes destructive of these ends, it is the Right of the People to alter or to abolish it, and to institute a new Government, laying its foundation on such principles and organizing its powers in such form, as to them shall seem most likely to effect their Safety and Happiness. Prudence, indeed, will dictate that Governments long established should not be changed for light and transient causes; and accordingly all experience hath shown, that mankind are more disposed to suffer, while evils are sufferable, than to right themselves by abolishing the forms to which they are accustomed. But when a long train of abuses and usurpations, pursuing invariably the same Object evinces a design to reduce them under absolute Despotism, it is their right, it is their duty, to throw off such Government, and to provide new Guards for their future security.—Such has been the patient sufferance of these Colonies: and such is now the necessity which constrains them to alter their former Systems of Government. The history of the present King of Great Britain is a history of repeated injuries and usurpations, all having in direct object the establishment of an absolute Tyranny over these States. To prove this, let Facts be submitted to a candid world.

Thomas Jefferson

Visual persuasion for unity . . .

Benjamin Franklin reflected the feeling of the colonists when he wrote a satire titled, "Exporting Felons to the Colonies," in which he suggested that the Americans should send shiploads of rattle-snakes to England in return for the human serpents Britain was so generously exporting to America.

The Snake Motif   Benjamin Franklin

The Liberty Song

Then join in hand brave Americans all,
By uniting we stand, by dividing we fall.

John Dickinson

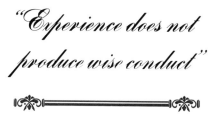

"Experience does not produce wise conduct"

"We learn from history that we learn nothing from history"

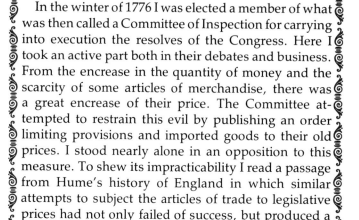

In the winter of 1776 I was elected a member of what was then called a Committee of Inspection for carrying into execution the resolves of the Congress. Here I took an active part both in their debates and business. From the encrease in the quantity of money and the scarcity of some articles of merchandise, there was a great encrease of their price. The Committee attempted to restrain this evil by publishing an order limiting provisions and imported goods to their old prices. I stood nearly alone in an opposition to this measure. To shew its impracticability I read a passage from Hume's history of England in which similar attempts to subject the articles of trade to legislative prices had not only failed of success, but produced a scarcity of provisions that bordered upon famine. The precedents of Mr. Hume had no effect upon the clamors that were urged in favor of the adoption of the measure, and it was finally carried by nearly an unanimous vote. I now saw that men do not become wise by the experience of other people. Subsequent observations taught me that even our own experience does not always produce wise conduct though the lessons for that purpose are sometimes repeated two or three times. With the best dispositions to act properly, the people of America imitated the blunders of nations in situations similar to their own, and scarcely succeeded in a single undertaking 'till they had exhausted all the errors that had been practiced in the same pursuits in other countries.

Benjamin Rush, 1776

 Do you believe this sort of attitude and behavior are still prevalent in America?

Write a paragraph similar to Rush's in which you undertake to convince people to change an attitude or mode of behavior that you regard as fairly common today.

Explaining the Crisis

These are the times that try men's souls. The summer soldier and the sunshine patriot will, in this crisis, shrink from the service of their country; but he that stands it *now*, deserves the love and thanks of man and woman. Tyranny, like hell, is not easily conquered; yet we have this consolation with us, that the harder the conflict, the more glorious the triumph. What we obtain too cheap, we esteem too lightly: it is dearness only that gives every thing its value. Heaven knows how to put a proper price upon its goods; and it would be strange indeed if so celestial an article as FREEDOM should not be highly rated. Britain, with an army to enforce her tyranny, has declared that she has a right (*not only to* TAX) but "To BIND *us in* ALL CASES WHATSOEVER," and if being *bound in that manner*, is not slavery, then is there not such a thing as slavery upon earth. Even the expression is impious; for so unlimited a power can belong only to God.

. . .

I have as little superstition in me as any man living, but my secret opinion has ever been, and still is, that God Almighty will not give up a people to military destruction, or leave them unsupportedly to perish, who have so earnestly and so repeatedly sought to avoid the calamities of war, by every decent method which wisdom could invent. Neither have I so much of the infidel in me, as to suppose that He has relinquished the government of the world, and given us up to the care of devils: and as I do not, I cannot see on what grounds the king of Britain can look up to heaven for help against us: a common murderer, a highwayman, or a house-breaker, has as good a pretence as he.

Thomas Paine, December 23, 1776

The second sentence of the first paragraph of this famous argument for continuing the Revolutionary War is quoted very frequently. What do you think makes it so memorable?

Write a similar sentence, employing Paine's rhythm and other techniques. Make your sentence refer to a current situation, one which you feel people should be encouraged to continue.

_____

_____

_____

_____

_____

_____

_____

_____

_____

_____

111

Tom Paine, master propagandist

Thomas Paine was the recipient of venomous hatred from many circles. It was fashionable to wear Tom Paine shoe nails so that he could be trampled underfoot. Tom Paine jugs were sold with painted snakes and Tom Paine's head on them. The jugs bore this inscription:

Observe the wicked and malicious man
Projecting all the mischief that he can.

On the other hand, he was honored and celebrated on many occasions.

Without the pen of Paine, the sword of Washington would have been wielded in vain.

John Adams

The Crisis appeared first in the *Pennsylvania Journal* of December 19, 1776. On the 23rd, it was published as a pamphlet. This is the title page of the first printing.

COMMON SENSE;

ADDRESSED TO THE

INHABITANTS

OF

AMERICA,

On the following interesting

SUBJECTS.

I. Of the Origin and Design of Government in general, with concise Remarks on the English Constitution.

II. Of Monarchy and Hereditary Succession.

III. Thoughts on the present State of American Affairs.

IV. Of the present Ability of America, with some miscellaneous Reflections.

Man knows no Master save creaing HEAVEN,
Or those whom choice and common good ordain.
THOMSON.

PHILADELPHIA;
Printed, and Sold, by R. BELL, in Third-Street.
MDCCLXXVI.

Stanzas

On the decease of Thomas Paine, who died at New York,
on the 8th of June, 1809

Princes and kings decay and die
   And, instant, rise again:
But this is not the case, trust me,
   With men like THOMAS PAINE.

In vain the democratic host
   His *equal* would attain:
For years to come they will not boast
   A second Thomas Paine.

Though many may his name assume;
   Assumption is in vain;
For every man has not *his* plume—
   Whose name is *Thomas Paine.*

Though heaven bestow'd on all its sons
   Their *proper* share of brain,
It gives to few, ye simple ones,
   The mind of Thomas Paine.

To tyrants and the tyrant crew,
   Indeed, he was the bane;
He writ, and gave them all their due,
   And signed it,—THOMAS PAINE.

Oh! how we loved to see him write
   And curb the race of Cain!
They hope and wish that Thomas P——
   May never rise again.

What idle hopes!—yes—such a man
   May yet appear again.—
When *they* are dead, they die for aye:
   —Not so with Thomas Paine.

Philip Freneau, 1809

113

VELUTI IN SPECULUM

To His Excellency General Washington

This plate is humbly Addressed by His Obedient Servant Thomas Tradeless

Oh, Washington is there not some chosen Curse; Some Hidden Thunder in the stores of Heaven,
Red with uncommon Wrath, to Blast those MEN Who owe their Greatness to their Country's RUIN?

The able Doctor. or America Swallowing the Bitter Draught.

British authority

Although Congress, whom the misguided *Americans* suffer to direct their opposition to a re-establishment of the constitutional government of these provinces, have disavowed every purpose of reconciliation not consonant with their *extravagant and inadmissable claim of Independence,* the King's Commissioners think fit to declare that they are equally desirous to confer with his Majesty's well-affected subjects upon the means of restoring the public tranquillity, and establishing a permanent union with every colony as a part of the British empire. . . . It is recommended to the inhabitants at large to reflect seriously upon their present condition and expectations, and judge for themselves whether it would be more inconsistent with their honor and happiness to offer up their lives as a sacrifice to the *unjust and precarious cause* in which they are engaged in, or return to their allegiance, accept the blessings of peace, and to be secured in a free enjoyment of their liberties and properties.

Lord Howe, 1776

Americans were bombarded with propaganda from their own leaders and from the British. Here are two brief examples.

Analyze the passages and write down the appeals in each.

versus

Congress

Commissioners, at the head of *fleets* and *armies* were sent to restore *peace* to America. After their arrival they issued a proclamation containing a promise of pardon. A pardon implies a precedent crime. What crime was it which the pardon so graciously proffered was meant to extinguish? That of refusing to surrender your birthright and to be bound, in all cases, by the acts of the British parliament. To receive a pardon was to acknowledge that asserting the essential rights of freemen was criminal; and to promise never to assert them any more. . . .

No middle line can now be drawn. Absolute and unconditional submission to their power is the end, long intended. . . . Absolute and unconditional submission! These are terms to which your ears have been unaccustomed. It behooves you fully to understand their meaning. . . . The horrors of *Asiatic* slavery rush into your views. . . . You would be numbered among slaves. . . .

To the Inhabitants of the United States, 1777

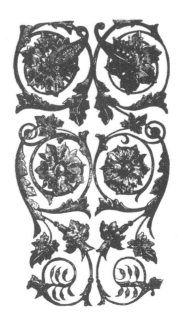

Lexington: one event, two points of view . . .

American Version

At Lexington . . . a company of militia . . . mustered near the meeting house. The [British] troops came in sight of them just before sunrise; and running within a few rods of them, the Commanding Officer [Pitcairn] accosted the militia in words to this effect: "Disperse, you rebels—damn you, throw down your arms and disperse"; upon which the troops huzzaed, and immediately one or two officers discharged their pistols, which were instantaneously followed by the firing of four or five of the soldiers, and then there seemed to be a general discharge from the whole body. Eight of our men were killed and nine wounded. . . .

. . . They pillaged almost every house they passed. . . . But the savage barbarity exercised upon the bodies of our unfortunate brethren who fell is almost incredible. Not contented with shooting down the unarmed, aged, and infirm, they disregarded the cries of the wounded, killing them. . . and mangling their bodies in the most shocking manner.

Salem, Mass., *Gazette,* **1775**

British Version

. . . Six companies of [British] light infantry . . . at Lexington found a body of the country people under arms, on a green close to the road. And upon the King's troops marching up to them, in order to inquire the reason of their being so assembled, they went off in great confusion. And several guns were fired upon the King's troops from behind a stone wall, and also from the meeting-house and other houses, by which one man was wounded, and Major Pitcairn's horse shot in two places. In consequence of this attack by the rebels, the troops returned the fire and killed several of them. . . .

On the return of the troops from Concord, they [the rebels] . . . began to fire upon them from behind stone walls and houses, and kept up in that manner a scattering fire during the whole of their march of fifteen miles, by which means several were killed and wounded. And such was the cruelty and barbarity of the rebels that they scalped and cut off the ears of some of the wounded men who fell into their hands.

London *Gazette,* **1775**

"The shot heard round the world..."

Battle of Lexington, April 19th 1775 Plate I.

 Write a comparison of the two reports. On what points do they appear to agree and disagree? Can you tell from examining both items the areas where probable truth lies?

Broadsides and bullets . . .

PROSPECT HILL	BUNKER'S HILL
I. Seven Dollars a Month.	*I. Three Pence a Day.*
II. Fresh Provisions, and in Plenty.	*II. Rotten Salt Pork.*
III. Health.	*III. The Scurvy.*
IV. Freedom, Ease, Affluence and a good Farm.	*IV. Slavery, Beggary and Want.*

To compare the situation of the Americans and their opponents, propaganda leaflets, such as the above, were wrapped around bullets and heaved into the British entrenchments on Bunker's Hill with the hope that the soldiers would see them before their officers could destroy them.

Tory propaganda in America . . .

 Assume you are one of the Sons of Liberty. Write a reply to one or both of these passages.

BUT REMEMBER:—your liberties and properties are now at the mercy of a body of men unchecked, uncontrolled by the civil power. You have chosen your committee;—you are no longer your own masters:—you have subjected your business, your dealings, your mode of living, the conduct and regulation of your families, to *their* prudence and discretion. . . . Violence is done to private property, by riotous assemblies, and the rioters go unpunished; nay more;—are applauded for those very crimes which the laws of the government have forbidden under severe penalties . . . *You* that spurned at the thought of holding your rights on the precarious tenure of the *will* of a British ministry . . . can *you* submit to hold them on as precarious a tenure, the *will* of a New York committee, of a Continental Congress?

Samuel Seabury
The Congress Canvassed

It is a remark that the high sons of Liberty consist of but two sorts of men. The first are those who by their debaucheries and ill conduct in life, are reduced almost to poverty, and are happy in finding a subsistence, though it is even on the destruction of their country; for on the turbulence of the times, and the heated imaginations of the populace, depends their existence. The latter are the ministers of the gospel, who, instead of preaching to their flocks meekness, sobriety, attention to their different employments, and a steady obedience to the laws of Britain, belch from the pulpit liberty, independence, and a steady perseverance in endeavoring to shake off their allegiance to the mother country.

New York *Gazeteer*, 1775

These excerpts are from ballads written by people opposed to the leaders of the Revolutionary movement.

Imagine you are back in that period, but in favor of the Revolution. Write a short ballad imitating the style and approach used here. But in your ballad, attack George III and the British military.

Would you know what a Whig is, and always was,
I'll show you his face, as it were in a glass,
He's a *rebel* by nature, a villain in grain,
A *saint* by profession, who never had grace:
Cheating and *lying* are puny things,
Raping and *plundering* venial sins,
His great occupation is ruining *nations*,
Subverting of Crowns, and *murdering Kings*.

New York *Gazeteer*

BRITANIA And Her DAUGHTER.

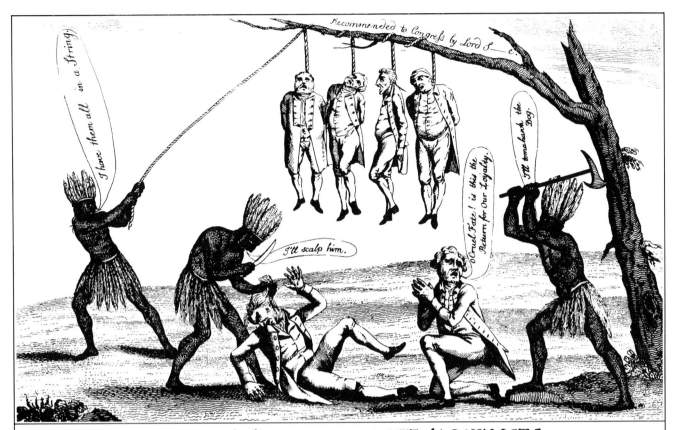

The SAVAGES let loose, OR The Cruel FATE of the LOYALISTS.

Is this a Peace, when Loyalists must bleed? It is a Bloody Piece of work ind.

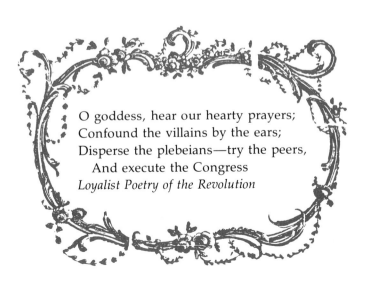

O goddess, hear our hearty prayers;
Confound the villains by the ears;
Disperse the plebeians—try the peers,
And execute the Congress
Loyalist Poetry of the Revolution

The Men deprav'd, who quit their Sphere,
Without Remorse, or Shame, or Fear,
And boldly rush, they know not where;
Seduc'd, alas! by fond Applause,
Of gaping Mobs, and loud Huzzas.
Unconscious all, of nobler Aim,
Than sordid Pelf, or vulgar Fame;
Men undefin'd by any Rules,
Ambiguous Things, half Knaves, half Fools,
Whom God denied the Talents great
Requir'd, to make a Knave, complete;
Whom Nature form'd, vile paltry Tools,
Absurder much, than downright Fools,
Who from their own dear Puppet-Show,
The World's great Stage, pretend to know.
The Patriots of North America

Persuasion for Canada . . .

The war of words between the
Americans and the British reached
into Canada where each side sought
support for its cause from Indians
and the military alike.

British General Carleton in Canada,
who was angered by American
propaganda brought to him by an
emissary, issued this order to his
subordinate officers:

. . . that letters or messages from rebels, traitors
in arms against their King, rioters, disturbers of
the peace, plunderers, robbers, assassins or mur-
derers, are on no occasion to be admitted. That
should emissaries of such lawless men again presume to approach the army, whether under the
name of flag-of-truce men or ambassadors, except
when they come to implore the King's mercy, their
persons shall be immediately seized and committed to close confinement, in order to be pro-
ceeded against as the law directs; their papers and
letters for whomsoever, even for the Commander-
in-Chief, are to be delivered to the Provost Mar-
shal, that, unread and unopened, they may be
burned by the hands of the common hangman.

General Washington wrote this
threatening letter to a tribe of
Canadian Indians in December 1776.

BROTHERS: I have a piece of news to tell you
which I hope you will attend to. Our enemy, the
King of Great Britain, endeavoured to stir up all
the Indians from Canada to South Carolina against
us. But our brethren of the Six Nations and their
allies the Shawanese and Delawares, would not
harken to the advice of the messengers sent among
them, but kept fast hold of our ancient convenant
chain. The Cherokees and Southern tribes were
foolish enough to listen to them, and to take up the
hatchet against us; upon which our warriors went
into their country, burnt their houses, destroyed
their corn, and obliged them to sue for peace and
give hostages for their future good behavior.

The British authorities wrote this to the Indians in 1777.

The King's army is victorious everywhere, and the rebels who bragged so much of their valor, fly before him like the deer before wolves and tigers. Their great army is dispersed and not finding protection in their strong forts and walls, have sought [safety] in inglorious flight. This we may reasonably expect will soon bring about a peace.

THE REPEAL. — or the Funeral Procession, of MISS AMERIC-STAMP.

The English argue among themselves . . .

Many Englishmen of the time felt that the Americans had good reasons for their anger. Some British leaders even argued for conciliation with the Americans.

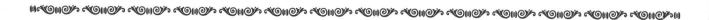

Here is an excerpt from a speech, "On American Taxation," by Edmund Burke, a British parliamentary orator.

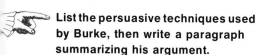

List the persuasive techniques used by Burke, then write a paragraph summarizing his argument.

LET US, SIR, embrace some system or other before we end this session. Do you mean to tax America, and to draw a productive revenue from thence? If you do, speak out: name, fix, ascertain this revenue; settle its quantity; define its objectives; provide for its collection; and then fight, when you have something to fight for. If you murder, rob; if you kill, take possession; and do not appear in the character of madmen as well as assassins, violent, vindictive, bloody, and tyrannical, without an object. But may better counsels guide you!

Again, and again, revert to your old principles,—seek peace and ensue it,—leave America, if she has taxable matter in her, to tax herself. I am not here going into the distinctions of rights, nor attempting to mark their boundaries. I do not enter into these metaphysical distinctions; I hate the very sound of them. Leave the Americans as they anciently stood, and these distinctions, born of our unhappy contest, will die along with it. They and we, and their and our ancestors, have been happy under that system. Let the memory of all actions in contradiction to that good old mode, on both sides, be extinguished forever. Be content to bind America by laws of trade: you have always done it. Let this be your reason for binding their trade. Do not burden them by taxes: you were not used to do so from the beginning. Let this be your reason for not taxing. These are the arguments of states and kingdoms. Leave the rest to the schools; for there only they may be discussed with safety. But if, intemperately, unwisely, fatally, you sophisticate and poison the very source of government, by urging subtle deductions, and consequences odious to those you govern, from the unlimited and illimitable nature of supreme sovereignty, you will teach them by these means to call that sovereignty itself in question. When you drive him hard, the boar will surely turn upon the hunters. If that sovereignty and their freedom cannot be reconciled, which will they take? They will cast your sovereignty in your face. Nobody will be argued into slavery. Sir, let the

ONY MAKING AT BOSTON

published in London 1774

gentlemen on the other side call forth all their ability; let the best of them get up and tell me what one character of liberty the Americans have, and what one brand of slavery they are free from, if they are bound in their property and industry by all the restraints you can imagine on commerce, and at the same time are made pack-horses of every tax you choose to impose, without the least share in granting them. When they bear the burdens of unlimited monopoly, will you bring them to bear the burdens of unlimited revenue too? The Englishman in America will feel that this is slavery: that it is *legal* slavery will be no compensation either to his feelings or his understanding.

The persuasive arguments of parliamentary speakers, such as Edmund Burke, did not prevail. The British press roused national pride to the point where most people believed that Britain ought to maintain its supremacy over the American colonies, that the behavior of the Bostonians was disgraceful. The following is typical of the official British position:

What then, is the present case? The supreme legislature of the whole British Empire has laid a duty (no matter for the present whether it has or has not a right to do so, it is sufficient that we conceive it has) . . . the people of America, at Boston particularly, resist that authority and oppose the execution of the law in a manner clearly treasonable upon the principles of every government upon earth. The mother country very unwilling to proceed to extremities passes laws (indisputably within its power) for the punishment of the most flagrant offenders, for the reformation of abuses, and for the prevention of the like enormities for the future. The question then is, whether these laws are to be submitted to: if the people of America say no, they say in effect that they will no longer be a part of the British Empire; they change the whole ground of the controversy; they no longer contend that Parliament has not a right to exact a particular provision, they say that it has no right to consider them at all as within its jurisdiction.

Dartmouth

125

George III analyzes the situation . . .

George III wrote this letter to his
prime minister, Lord North, on June
11, 1779. In it he expresses fears
about the possibility of American
independence. What is he concerned
about? Did his reservations turn
out to be valid?

 Write a short essay that provides
the historical perspective to
George III's letter.

I *should think it the greatest instance of the many I have met with of ingratitude and injustice, if it could be supposed that any man in my dominions more ardently desired the restoration of peace and solid happiness in every part of this empire than I do. There is no personal sacrifice I could not readily yield for so desirable an object, but at the same time no inclination to get out of the present difficulties, which certainly keep my mind very far from a state of ease, can incline me to enter into what I look upon as the destruction of the Empire. I have heard Lord North frequently drop that the advantages to be gained by this contest could never repay the expence. I own that let any war be ever so successful they will find as in the last that it has impoverished the State, enriched individuals, and perhaps raised the name only of the conquerors, but this is only weighing such events in the scale of a tradesman behind his counter. It is necessary for those in the station it has pleased Divine Providence to place me in to weigh whether expences though very great are not sometimes necessary to prevent what might be more ruinous to a country than the loss of money. The present contest with America I cannot help seeing as the most serious in which any country was ever engaged. It contains such a train of consequences that they must be examined to feel its real weight. Whether the laying a tax was deserving all the evils that have arisen from it, I should suppose no man could allege that without being more fit for Bedlam than a seat in the senate; but step by step the demands of America have risen—independence is their object, that certainly is one that every man not willing to sacrifice every object to a* momentary and inglorious *peace must concur with me in thinking that this country can never submit to. Should America succeed in that the West Indies must follow them. . . . Ireland would soon follow the same plan and be a separate state. Then this island would be a poor island indeed, for reduced in her trade merchants would retire with their wealth to climates more to their advantage, and shoals of manufacturers would leave this country for the new Empire.*
. . . Consequently this country has but one sensible, one great line to follow, the being ever ready to make peace when to be obtained without submitting to terms that in their consequence must annihilate this empire, and with firmness to make every effort to deserve success.

Looking Back at Revolutionary Propaganda

Here are two statements from different sources referring to propaganda used in the American Revolutionary War.

What does each tell us about the significance of propaganda in those times?

Compare one statement with the other. Do they essentially cover the same points, or are there differences? Write an essay that reflects your answer to the question.

"From the inception of the controversy," Professor Schlesinger has stated, "the patriots exhibited extraordinary skill in manipulating public opinion, playing upon the emotions of the ignorant as well as the minds of the educated."

As propagandists, the Americans demonstrated great ability. Understanding the uses to which the printing press could be put, they embarked on devastating attacks on the "sceptered savage of Great Britain," who was charged, by one writer, with a thirst "for the blood of America. Hessians, Hanoverians, Brunswickers, Canadians, Indians, Negroes, Regulars and Tories are invited to the carnage."

That these people actually became involved in the war was no exaggeration, but their activities did little service to England. The Americans, stirred to greater resistance, countered not only with arms but with the propaganda and subversive operations that we have described.

As to these latter activities, the leaders of the Revolution, even in the midst of their most angry flood of words, never lost sight of the fact that they were no substitute for military power. Speaking of this and the search for peace, John Adams wrote in 1781 that only Washington and Greene "and their colleagues in the army" could truly negotiate for America. The British government, which sent armies and fleets to America to persuade the Americans to forego rebellion and independence, ended up being persuaded to relinquish the colonies—persuaded by the stubborn resistance of Washington, Greene, "their colleagues in the army," and the potent French alliance.

Carl Berger

The work of the propagandists has spoken for itself; by their fruits we have known them. Without their work independence would not have been declared in 1776 nor recognized in 1783.

British legislation was, of course, the immediate occasion for rebellion. The provincial ruling class, threatened in its position, used legal agencies of government and already established social institutions to undermine and ultimately to overthrow the British control. Through propaganda they spread the alarm to all classes. The propagandists identified the interests of the provincial ruling class with national interests and created a war psychosis. It was the propagandists who made inchoate feelings articulate opinion and provided the compulsive ideals which led to concrete action.

A movement originating in the necessities of the provincial class thus became in the capable hands of its leaders a dominant national movement. The ideas and interests of those who wished to remain within the empire were ultimately overwhelmed and their leaders discredited by patriot propaganda, but not before the pro-British advocates had made an effective counterattack.

As a result, much of what we know of the Revolution has been learned from revolutionary propaganda. The patriots were not all of the lower classes, frontiersmen and buckskins as Tory propaganda had it; the friends of England were not all aristocrats and oppressors of the down-trodden, as Whig propaganda had it. Nationalism was not the cause of the revolution, nor was it democratic in its origin, but the work of the revolutionary propagandists aided in developing the feeling of nationalism and in stimulating the ideals of a new democracy.

The propagandists thus gave expression to ideals that had been germinating for years; the appeals to a common history and a common destiny and the ideas they presented expressed clearly what the people had but dimly sensed. The fears the propagandists aroused and the hopes they enkindled became the national fears and national hopes. The national ideals of American life, slowly maturing through the colonial period, thus came clearly into the consciousness of the American people through the effects of war propaganda.

Philip Davidson

A message for Europeans—selling the new nation . . .

He is an AMERICAN, who, leaving behind him all his ancient prejudices and manners, receives new ones from the new mode of life he has embraced, the new government he obeys, and the new rank he holds. He becomes an American by being received in the broad lap of our great *Alma Mater.* Here individuals of all nations are melted into a new race of men, whose labours and posterity will one day cause great changes in the world. Americans are the western pilgrims, who are carrying along with them that great mass of arts, sciences, vigour, and industry which began long since in the east; they will finish the great circle. The Americans were once scattered all over Europe; here they are incorporated into one of the finest systems of population which has ever appeared, and which will hereafter become distinct by the power of the different climates they inhabit. The American ought therefore to love this country much better than that wherein either he or his forefathers were born. Here the rewards of his industry follow with equal steps the progress of his labour; his labour is founded on the basis of nature, *self-interest;* can it want a stronger allurement? Wives and children, who before in vain demanded of him a morsel of bread, now, fat and frolicsome, gladly help their father to clear those fields whence exuberant crops are to arise to feed and to clothe them all; without any part being claimed, either by a despotic prince, a rich abbot, or a mighty lord. Here religion demands but little of him; a small voluntary salary to the minister, and gratitude to God; can he refuse these? The American is a new man, who acts upon new principles; he must therefore entertain new ideas, and form new opinions. From involuntary idleness, servile dependence, penury, and useless labour, he has passed to toils of a very different nature, rewarded by ample subsistence.—This is an American.

Michel-Guillaume Jean De Crèvecoeur, 1782

130

Put on your tricornered hat and write an advertisement for the London *Herald* **of March 15, 1790, urging people to move to the newest nation in the world and to make their home here.**

Now write an advertisement which will be published next March 15, urging Londoners to settle in today's USA.

Of course, your arguments and language will differ. Will you also use different persuasive techniques? State the reasons for your decision.

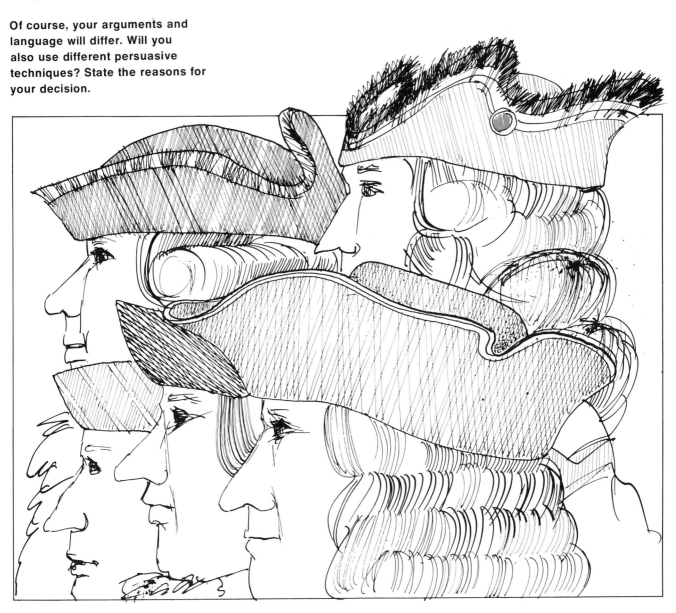

A prophecy!

Columbia

Columbia, Columbia, to glory arise,
The queen of the world, and child of the skies!
Thy genius commands thee; with rapture behold,
While ages on ages thy splendors unfold.
Thy reign is the last, and the noblest of time,
Most fruitful thy soil, most inviting thy clime;
Let the crimes of the east ne'er encrimson thy name.
Be freedom, and science, and virtue, thy fame.

To conquest, and slaughter, let Europe aspire;
Whelm nations in blood, and wrap cities in fire;
Thy heroes the rights of mankind shall defend,
And triumph pursue them, and glory attend.
A world is thy realm: for a world be thy laws,
Enlarg'd as thine empire, and just as thy cause;
On Freedom's broad basis, that empire shall rise,
Extend with the main, and dissolve with the skies.

Timothy Dwight, 1777

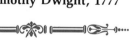

Imagine that Freneau could return to your part of the United States. Write a passage that you think would reflect his feelings today.

*I*t is not easy to conceive what will be the greatness and importance of North America in a century or two to come, if the present fabric of Nature is upheld, and the people retain those bold and manly sentiments of freedom, which actuate them at this day. Agriculture, the basis of a nation's greatness, will here, most probably, be advanced to its summit of perfection; and its attendant, commerce, will so agreeably and usefully employ mankind, that wars will be forgotten; nations, by a free intercourse with this vast and fertile continent, and this continent with the whole world, will again become brothers after so many centuries of hatred and jealousy, and no longer treat each other as savages and monsters. The iron generation will verge to decay, and those days of felicity advance which have been so often wished for by all good men, and which are so beautifully described by the prophetic sages of ancient times.

Philip Freneau, 1782

The British surrendering their Arms to Gen: Washington after their defeat at York Town in Virginia October 1781.

Revolution: blessing or curse?

. . . yet, it appears to me there is an option still left to the United States of America, that it is in their choice, and depends upon their conduct, whether they will be respectable and prosperous, or comtemptible and miserable as a Nation. This is the time of their political probation, this is the moment when the eyes of the whole World are turned upon them, this is the moment to establish or ruin their national Character forever, this is the favorable moment to give such a tone to our Federal Government, as will enable it to answer the ends of its institution, or this may be the ill-fated moment for relaxing the powers of the Union, annihilating the cement of the Confederation, and exposing us to become the sport of European politics, which may play one State against another to prevent their growing importance, and to serve their own interested purposes. For, according to the system of Policy the States shall adopt at this moment, they will stand or fall, and by their confirmation or lapse, it is yet to be decided, whether the Revolution must ultimately be considered as a blessing or a curse: a blessing or a curse, not to the present age alone, for with our fate will the destiny of unborn Millions be involved. . . .

I now make it my earnest prayer, that God would have you, and the State over which you preside, in his holy protection, that he would incline the hearts of the Citizens to cultivate a spirit of subordination and obedience to Government, to entertain a brotherly affection and love for one another, for their fellow Citizens of the United States at large, and particularly for their brethren who have served in the Field. . . .

George Washington, 1783

Rip Van Winkle wakes up to a new country . . .

Here is a fictional account of the changes made by the Revolution, written 44 years after the event. This is the scene of Rip Van Winkle's return to his village after his magical sleep on the mountainside.

Do you note a bias in Irving's description? Which side is _he_ on? Does he admire the "new" busy, bustling American, or is he nostalgic for the good old Colonial days? Or is he neutral? List words, phrases, sentences of the excerpt that led you to your decision.

Instead of the great tree that used to shelter the quiet little Dutch inn of yore, there now was reared a tall naked pole, with something on the top that looked like a red nightcap, and from it was fluttering a flag, on which was a singular assemblage of stars and stripes:—all this was strange and incomprehensible. He recognized on the sign, however, the ruby face of King George, under which he had smoked so many a peaceful pipe; but even this was singularly metamorphosed. The red coat was changed for one of blue and buff, a sword was held in the hand instead of a sceptre, the head was decorated with a cocked hat, and underneath was painted in large characters, GENERAL WASHINGTON.

There was, as usual, a crowd of folk about the door, but none that Rip recollected. The very character of the people seemed changed. There was a busy, bustling, disputatious tone about it, instead of the accustomed phlegm and drowsy tranquility. He looked in vain for the sage Nicholas Vedder, with his broad face, double chin, and fair long pipe, uttering clouds of tobacco-smoke instead of idle speeches; or Van Bummel, the schoolmaster, doling forth the contents of an ancient newspaper. In place of these, a lean, bilious-looking fellow, with his pockets full of hand-bills, was haranguing vehemently about rights of citizens—elections—members of congress—liberty—Bunker's Hill —heroes of seventy-six—and other words, which were a perfect Babylonish jargon to the bewildered Van Winkle.

The appearance of Rip, with his long, grizzled beard, his rusty fowling-piece, his uncouth dress, and an army of women and children at his heels, soon attracted the attention of the tavern-politicians. They crowded round him, eying him from head to foot with great curiosity. The orator bustled up to him, and, drawing him partly aside, inquired "On which side he voted?" Rip stared in vacant stupidity. Another short but busy little fellow pulled him by the arm, and, rising on tiptoe, inquired in his ear, "Whether he was Federal or Democrat?" Rip was equally at a loss to comprehend the question; when a knowing, self-important old gentleman, in a sharp cocked hat, made his way through the crowd, putting them to the right and left with his elbows as he passed, and planting himself before Van Winkle, with one arm akimbo, the other resting on his cane, his keen eyes and sharp hat penetrating, as it were, into his very soul, demanded, in an austere tone, "What brought him to the election with a gun on his shoulder, and a mob at his heels; and whether he meant to breed a riot in the village?"—"Alas! gentlemen," cried Rip, somewhat dismayed, "I am a poor quiet man, a native of the place, and a loyal subject of the King, God bless him!"

Here a general shout burst from the by-standers—"A tory! a tory! a spy! a refugee! hustle him! away with him!" It was with great difficulty that the self-important man in the cocked hat restored order; and, having assumed a tenfold austerity of brow, demanded again of the unknown culprit, what he came there for, and whom he was seeking? The poor man humbly assured him that he meant no harm, but merely came there in search of some of his neighbors, who used to keep about the tavern.

Washington Irving, 1820

The Constitution: A New Propaganda Battle

After the thirteen states won independence from Great Britain, a great debate ensued over acceptance of the proposed Constitution. People were concerned about the role of the President, the rights of the individual states, how united the United States should be, the rights of the citizens, slavery, the choice of legislators, and many other questions.

Here are some of the arguments put forth at that momentous time. Do they seem persuasive to you? Explain why.

Write a carefully supported argument which undertakes to prove that *one* of these positions is wrong.

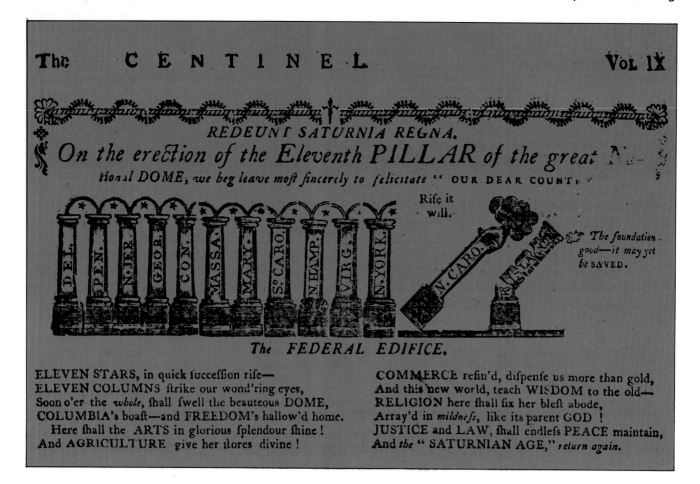

The CENTINEL   Vol IX

REDEUNT SATURNIA REGNA.

On the erection of the Eleventh PILLAR of the great National DOME, we beg leave most sincerely to felicitate "OUR DEAR COUNTRY."

Rise it will.

The foundation good—it may yet be SAVED.

The FEDERAL EDIFICE.

ELEVEN STARS, in quick succession rise—
ELEVEN COLUMNS strike our wond'ring eyes,
Soon o'er the *whole*, shall swell the beauteous DOME,
COLUMBIA's boast—and FREEDOM's hallow'd home.
   Here shall the ARTS in glorious splendour shine!
And AGRICULTURE give her stores divine!

COMMERCE refin'd, dispense us more than gold,
And this new world, teach WISDOM to the old—
RELIGION here shall fix her blest abode,
Array'd in *mildness*, like its parent GOD!
JUSTICE and LAW, shall endless PEACE maintain,
And *the* "SATURNIAN AGE," *return again*.

This Constitution is said to have beautiful features; but when I come to examine these features, sir, they appear to me horribly frightful. Among other deformities, it has an awful squinting; it squints towards monarchy; and does not this raise indignation in the breast of every true American?

Your President may easily become king. Your Senate is so imperfectly constructed that your dearest rights may be sacrificed by what may be a small minority; and a very small minority may continue forever unchangeably this government, although horridly defective. Where are your checks in this government? Your strongholds will be in the hands of your enemies. It is on a supposition that your American governors shall be honest, that all the good qualities of this government are founded, but its defective and imperfect construction puts it in their power to perpetrate the worst of mischiefs, should they be bad men; and, sir, would not all the world, from the eastern to the western hemisphere, blame our distracted folly in resting our rights upon the contingency of our rulers being good or bad? Show me that age and country where the rights and liberties of the people were placed on the sole chance of their rulers being good men, without a consequent loss of liberty! I say that the loss of that dearest privilege has ever followed, with absolute certainty, every such mad attempt.

Patrick Henry, 1788

The President of the United States would be liable to be impeached, tried, and, upon conviction of treason, bribery, or other high crimes or misdemeanors, removed from office; and would afterwards be liable to prosecution and punishment in the ordinary course of law. The person of the king of Great Britain is sacred and inviolable; there is no constitutional tribunal to which he is amenable; no punishment to which he can be subjected without involving the crisis of a national revolution. In this delicate and important circumstance of personal responsibility, the President of Confederated America would stand upon no better ground than a governor of New York, and upon worse ground than the governors of Maryland and Delaware.

Alexander Hamilton, 1788

The proposed Constitution, so far from implying an abolition of the State governments, makes them constituent parts of the national sovereignty, by allowing them a direct representation in the Senate, and leaves in their possession certain exclusive and very important portions of sovereign power. This fully corresponds, in every rational import of the terms, with the idea of a federal government.

Alexander Hamilton, 1787

PATRICK HENRY.

Here Franklin expresses misgivings about the Constitution, admits that it has faults. Is he doing so in order to use the persuasive technique he described in his autobiography? How do you know?

Is the sort of approach he takes in arguing for the Constitution ever used today? If you know of any examples, describe them. If not, describe some instance in which Franklin's approach might have been more effective than the one used.

In these sentiments, Sir, I agree to this Constitution, with all its faults,—if they are such; because I think a general Government necessary for us, and there is no form of government but what may be a blessing to the people, if well administered; and I believe, farther, that this is likely to be well administered for a course of years, and can only end in despotism, as other forms have done before it, when the people shall become so corrupted as to need despotic government, being incapable of any other. I doubt, too, whether any other Convention we can obtain, may be able to make a better constitution; for, when you assemble a number of men, to have the advantage of their joint wisdom, you inevitably assemble with those men all their prejudices, their passions, their errors of opinion, their local interests, and their selfish views. From such an assembly can a perfect production be expected? It therefore astonishes me, Sir, to find this system approaching so near to perfection as it does; and I think it will astonish our enemies, who are waiting with confidence to hear, that our councils are confounded like those of the builders of Babel, and that our States are on the point of separation, only to meet hereafter for the purpose of cutting one another's throats. Thus I consent, Sir, to this Constitution, because I expect no better, and because I am not sure that it is not the best.

Benjamin Franklin, 1787

138

From *The Autobiography*

While I was intent on improving my Language, I met with an English Grammar (I think it was Greenwood's) at the End of which there were two little Sketches of the Arts of Rhetoric and Logic, the latter finishing with a Specimen of a Dispute in the Socratic Method. And soon after I procur'd Xenophon's Memorable Things of Socrates, wherein there are many Instances of the same Method. I was charm'd with it, adopted it, dropt my abrupt Contradiction, and positive Argumentation, and put on the humble Enquirer and Doubter. And being then, from reading Shaftsbury and Collins, become a real Doubter in many Points of our Religious Doctrine, I found this Method safest for my self and very embarrassing to those against whom I used it, therefore I took a Delight in it, practis'd it continually and grew very artful and expert in drawing People even of superior Knowledge into Concessions the Consequences of which they did not foresee, entangling them in Difficulties out of which they could not extricate themselves, and so obtaining Victories that neither my self nor my Cause always deserved.

I continu'd this Method some few Years, but gradually left it, retaining only the Habit of expressing my self in Terms of modest Diffidence, never using when I advance any thing that may possibly be disputed, the Words, Certainly, undoubtedly, or any others that give the Air of Positiveness to an Opinion; but rather say, I conceive, or I apprehend a Thing to be so or so. It appears to me, or I should think it so or so for such and such Reasons, or I imagine it to be so, or it is so if I am not mistaken. This Habit I believe has been of great Advantage to me, when I have had occasion to inculcate my Opinions and persuade Men into Measures that I have been from time to time engag'd in promoting.

Benjamin Franklin, 1771–1789

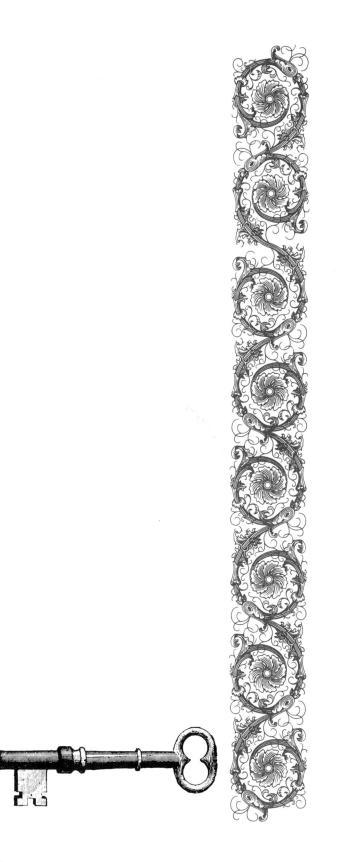

Paine's pen endorses the new government . . .

Thomas Paine wrote this glorification
of American ideals right after the
new nation had been established.

 Write a few paragraphs continuing
Paine's statement and bringing it
up to date.

 Write a short essay analyzing Paine's
propaganda: the arguments he
employs and the language he uses
to express them. Do you note
any fallacies?

The independence of America, considered merely as a separation from England, would have been a matter but of little importance, had it not been accompanied by a revolution in the principles and practice of governments. She made a stand, not for herself only, but for the world, and looked beyond the advantages herself could receive. Even the Hessian, though hired to fight against her, may live to bless his defeat: and England, condemning the viciousness of its government, rejoice in its miscarriage.

As America was the only spot in the political world where the principle of universal reformation could begin, so also was it the best in the natural world. An assemblage of circumstances conspired, not only to give birth, but to add gigantic maturity to its principles. The scene which that country presents to the eye of a spectator, has something in it which generates and encourages great ideas. Nature appears to him in magnitude. The mighty objects he beholds, act upon his mind by enlarging it, and he partakes of the greatness he contemplates.—Its first settlers were emigrants from different European nations, and of diversified professions of religion, retiring from the governmental persecutions of the old world, and meeting in the new, not as enemies, but as brothers. The wants which necessarily accompany the cultivation of a wilderness produced among them a state of society, which countries long harassed by the quarrels and intrigues of governments, had neglected to cherish. In such a situation man becomes what he ought. He sees his species, not with the inhuman idea of a natural enemy, but as kindred; and the example shews to the artificial world, that man must go back to Nature for information.

From the rapid progress which America makes in every species of improvement, it is rational to conclude that, if the governments of Asia, Africa, and Europe had begun on a principle similar to that of America, or had not been very early corrupted therefrom, those countries must by this time have been in a far superior condition to what they are. Age after

age has passed away, for no other purpose than to behold their wretchedness. Could we suppose a spectator who knew nothing of the world, and who was put into it merely to make his observations, he would take a great part of the old world to be new, just struggling with the difficulties and hardships of an infant settlement. He could not suppose that the hordes of miserable poor with which old countries abound could be any other than those who had not yet had time to provide for themselves. Little would he think they were the consequence of what in such countries they call government.

If, from the more wretched parts of the old world, we look at those which are in an advanced stage of improvement we still find the greedy hand of government thrusting itself into every corner and crevice of industry, and grasping the spoil of the multitude. Invention is continually exercised to furnish new pretences for revenue and taxation. It watches prosperity as its prey, and permits none to escape without a tribute.

Thomas Paine, 1791
From *Rights of Man*

Slavery, Slaves, and Propaganda

Much of the controversy over adopting the Constitution was caused by the desire of some delegates to abolish slavery, and the determination of others to continue it, at least in their own states. But the schism did not start there. Since the early British settling, the people of America have been concerned about the situation of the black people in the land. Until the Civil War, the dispute was carried on through spoken and written arguments that ranged from the most emotional to the most legalistic. All tried to persuade with words. A few samples of this extensive propaganda effort indicate its importance in the development of American attitudes.

Against slavery . . .

This excerpt is from the earliest American abolitionist propaganda, a pamphlet published in 1700 by Judge Samuel Sewall, who opposed slavery on religious, moral, and economic grounds.

Write a sentence imitating the first sentence of this selection. Then use it as the topic sentence of a paragraph or two arguing for improved treatment of a minority or ethnic group that lives at a disadvantage in the United States today.

The Selling of Joseph

A MEMORIAL

"For as much liberty is in real value next unto life: None ought to part with it themselves, or deprive others of it, but upon most mature consideration."

. . . It is likewise most lamentable to think how, in taking negroes out of Africa and selling of them here, that which God has joined together men do boldly rend asunder: men from their country, husbands from their wives, parents from their children. How horrible is the uncleanness, immorality, if not murder, that the ships are guilty of that bring great crowds of these miserable men and women! Methinks, when we are bemoaning the barbarous usage of our friends and kinsfolk in Africa, it might not be unseasonable to inquire whether we are not culpable in forcing the Africans to become slaves among ourselves. And it may be a question whether all the benefit received by negro slaves will balance the account of cash laid out upon them; and for the redemption of our own enslaved friends out of Africa. Besides all the persons and estates that have perished there.

. . . Christians should carry it to all the world, as the Israelites were to carry it one towards another. And for men obstinately to persist in holding their neighbors and brethren under the rigor of perpetual bondage, seems to be no proper way of gaining assurance that God has given them spiritual freedom. Our blessed Saviour has altered the measures of the ancient love-song, and set it to a most excellent new tune, which all ought to be ambitious of learning. Matt. v. 43, 44. John xii. 34. These Ethiopians, as black as they are, seeing they are the sons and daughters of the first Adam, the brethren and sisters of the last Adam, and the off-spring of God, they ought to be treated with a respect agreeable.

Samuel Sewall, 1700

There must doubtless be an unhappy influence on the manners of our people produced by the existence of slavery among us. The whole commerce between master and slave is a perpetual exercise of the most boisterous passions, the most unremitting despotism on the one part, and degrading submissions on the other. Our children see this, and learn to imitate it; for man is an imitative animal. This quality is the germ of all education in him. From his cradle to his grave he is learning to do what he sees others do. If a parent could find no motive either in his philanthropy or his self-love, for restraining the intemperance of passion towards his slave, it should always be a sufficient one that his child is present. But generally it is not sufficient. The parent storms, the child looks on, catches the lineaments of wrath, puts on the same airs in the circle of smaller slaves, gives a loose to the worst of passions, and thus nursed, educated, and daily exercised in tyranny, cannot but be stamped by it with odious peculiarities. The man must be a prodigy who can retain his manners and morals undepraved by such circumstances. And with what execration should the statesman be loaded, who, permitting one half the citizens thus to trample on the rights of the other, transforms those into despots, and these into enemies, destroys the morals of the one part, and the amor patriae of the other. For if a slave can have a country in this world, it must be any other in preference to that in which he is born to live and labor for another; in which he must lock up the faculties of his nature, contribute as far as depends on his individual endeavors to the evanish-

 On the basis of Jefferson's argument, discuss what he means by "Indeed I tremble for my country when I reflect that God is just."

ment of the human race, or entail his own miserable condition on the endless generations proceeding from him. With the morals of the people, their industry also is destroyed. For in a warm climate, no man will labor for himself who can make another labor for him. This is so true, that of the proprietors of slaves a very small proportion indeed are ever seen to labor. And can the liberties of a nation be thought secure when we have removed their only firm basis, a conviction in the minds of the people that these liberties are of the gift of God? They they are not to be violated but with His wrath? Indeed I tremble for my country when I reflect that God is just; that his justice cannot sleep forever; that considering numbers, nature and natural means only, a revolution of the wheel of fortune, an exchange of situation is among possible events; that it may become probable by supernatural interference! The Almighty has no attribute which can take side with us in such a contest. But it is impossible to be temperate and to pursue this subject through the various considerations of policy, of morals, of history natural and civil. We must be contented to hope they will force their way into every one's mind. I think a change already perceptible, since the origin of the present revolution. The spirit of the master is abating, that of the slave rising from the dust, his condition mollifying, the way I hope preparing, under the auspices of heaven, for a total emancipation, and that this is disposed, in the order of events, to be with the consent of the masters, rather than by their extirpation.

Thomas Jefferson, 1781
From *Notes on Virginia*

145

When Jefferson drafted the Declaration of Independence, he included this antislavery clause. It was omitted from the final version because the delegates could not reach even a compromise agreement on the issue of slavery.

He [George III] has waged cruel war against human nature itself, violating its most sacred rights of life and liberty in the persons of a distant people who never offended him, captivating and carrying them into slavery in another hemisphere, or to incur miserable death in their transportation thither. This piratical warfare, the opprobrium of infidel powers, is the warfare of the Christian King of Great Britain. Determined to keep open a market where MEN *should be bought and sold, he has prostituted his negative [royal veto] for suppressing every legislative attempt to prohibit or to restrain this execrable commerce. And that this assemblage of horrors might want no fact of distinguished dye [might lack no flagrant crime], he is now exciting those very people to rise in arms among us, and to purchase that liberty of which he has deprived them by murdering the people upon whom he also obtruded them: thus paying off former crimes committed against the liberties of one people with crimes which he urges them to commit against the lives of another.*

 Consider the wording of the anti-slavery clause. Is it as persuasive as the rest of the Declaration? In what ways? Do you think the arguments it offers were the cause of its rejection?

 Here is the reason Jefferson cited for Congress's omission of the antislavery clause:

The clause too, reprobating the enslaving the inhabitants of Africa, was struck out in complaisance to South Carolina and Georgia, who had never attempted to restrain the importation of slaves, and who, on the contrary, still wished to continue it. Our northern brethren also, I believe, felt a little tender under those censures; for though their people had very few slaves themselves, yet they had been pretty considerable carriers of them to others.

 On the basis of the two historical statements on this page, write an editorial, datelined Philadelphia 1775, urging George III to abolish slavery in the American colonies.

For slavery . . .

A landowner in Virginia supported slavery by equating it with the hard work required of day laborers in England. Write a paragraph showing that his defense has validity. Then write a paragraph opposing his argument.

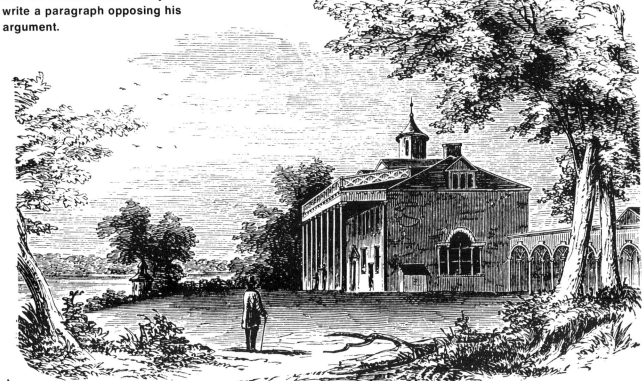

Because I have heard how strangely cruel, and severe, the Service of this Country is represented in some parts of *England;* I can't forbear affirming, that the work of their Servants, and Slaves, is no other than what every common Freeman do's. Neither is any Servant requir'd to do more in a Day, than his Overseer. And I can assure you with a great deal of Truth, that generally their Slaves are not worked near so hard, nor so many Hours in a Day, as the Husbandmen, and Day-Labourers in *England.*

Robert Beverly, 1705

Slavery debate at the Constitutional Convention . . .

> *Religion and humanity have nothing to do with this question. Interest alone is the governing principle with nations. The true question at present is whether the southern states shall or shall not be parties to the Union.*
> **John Rutledge**

> *Let us not intermeddle. As population increases, poor laborers will be so plentiful as to render slaves useless. Slavery in time will not be a speck in our country.*
> **Oliver Ellsworth**

TO BE SOLD on board the Ship *Bance-Ifland*, on tuefday the 6th of *May* next, at *Afhley-Ferry*; a choice cargo of about 250 fine healthy

NEGROES,

juft arrived from the **Windward & Rice Coaft.** —The utmoft care has already been taken, and fhall be continued, to keep them free from the leaft danger of being infected with the SMALL-POX, no boat having been on board, and all other communication with people from *Charles-Town* prevented.
Auftin, Laurens, & Appleby.

N. B. Full one Half of the above Negroes have had the SMALL-POX in their own Country.

An advertisement of a cargo of slaves aboard the Bance-Island, *anchored off Charleston, during a plague of smallpox.*

> *Slavery discourages arts and manufactures. The poor despise labor when performed by slaves. They prevent the immigration of whites, who really enrich and strengthen a country. They produce the most pernicious effect on manners. Every master of slaves is born a petty tyrant. They bring the judgement of heaven on a country. As nations can not be rewarded or punished in the next world they must be in this. By an inevitable chain of causes and effects providence punishes national sins by national calamities.*
> **George Mason**

TO EDWARD COLES

Monticello, August 25th, '14

DEAR SIR,—Your favour of July 31, was duly received, and was read with peculiar pleasure. The sentiments breathed through the whole do honor to both the head and heart of the writer. Mine on the subject of slavery of negroes have long since been in possession of the public, and time has only served to give them stronger root. The love of justice and the love of moral reproach to us that they should have pleaded it so long in vain, and should have produced not a single effort, nay I fear not much serious willingness to relieve them & ourselves from our present condition of moral & political reprobation. From those of the former generation who were in the fulness of age when I came into public life, which was while our controversy with England was on paper only, I soon saw that nothing was to be hoped. Nursed and educated in the daily habit of seeing the degraded condition, both bodily and mental, of those unfortunate beings, not reflecting that that degradation was very much the work of themselves & their fathers, few minds have yet doubted but that they were as legitimate subjects of property as their horses and cattle.

Thomas Jefferson

Viewed from the hindsight of history, which of the preceding slavery statements proved to be valid? Write a carefully reasoned essay in which you support your position by citing actual events in the development of the United States.

Making Use of the Propaganda of the Past

From these impressive beginnings during the period of the Revolution and the early Republic, Americans went on to develop ever greater skill in persuasion. There were many propaganda-filled eras in the development of the United States: the settling of the West and the wars against the Indians, the influx of immigrants from various European and Asian countries, the rise of the labor movement, and the campaign for woman suffrage, among others. Then, of course, extensive propaganda wars preceded and accompanied every military war. And each election day sees the close of intensive propaganda efforts.

There have been new developments in the techniques of persuasion, and the technology has greatly improved. But there also is much consistency in propaganda appeals.

Now that you have had a close look at the propaganda of one era, you understand what to seek and how to analyze the propaganda of other periods. Here are some projects designed to help you apply the insights you have gained and the techniques you have learned.

1 Slavery continued to be the subject of propaganda barrages until the mid-nineteenth century when this issue, too, was resolved with bullets and bayonets. But the end of black slavery did not mark the end of racial problems in the United States. Read some articles about the position of the black people in America after the Civil War. Then read some articles about contemporary race relations, and note which arguments they have in common with the eighteenth- and nineteenth-century materials you have read.

Write an essay analyzing those logical fallacies that appear frequently in arguments about the relationship of the black and white races.

2 Choose some period of history that interests you: the Roman era, the Elizabethan period in England, the times of the Pilgrims in America, the American Revolution, the expansion of the American West. Do enough research so that you know something about the times, then select a relevant topic, such as "land opportunities on the Prairies," and write a brochure designed to move your reader into some action that you have planned for him.

3

Read some of the pro and con arguments on either the passage of the Nineteenth Amendment to the U.S. Constitution or on allowing the admission of foreigners to this country. On the basis of what you know (or read) about sexual or ethnic prejudice today, consider the validity of those arguments. Discuss which earlier predictions came true. If you had lived at that time, which argument would have persuaded you?

Write a short pamphlet urging people to adopt your method of solving a single identifiable problem of sexual or ethnic animosity in the United States today. Prepare a complete layout for your pamphlet, including either illustrations or descriptions of suitable illustrations and their placement. Make the whole as persuasive as possible.

4

"At all times, most public events are experienced vicariously."
Henry M. Pachter

Discuss this statement with a group of classmates, and compile a list of the ways in which public events were communicated during earlier historical periods. Then consider the view of reality presented by each method.

Today, we still experience public events vicariously, but we do so much more promptly than did our ancestors. In fact, sometimes we experience events while they are happening, even though—as in the case of the moon landing shown on TV—we are millions of miles away. Is our view of reality the same or different from that of our ancestors because our technology is better? Write a discussion of this idea in a well-focused essay.

Are people today more or less gullible than those of the past? What evidence is there to support your opinion?

5

The year is 2276. You are a wise anthropologist who has just excavated the ruins of the community in which you are located as you read this page. For a long while, you uncover only buildings. Finally, you discover . . . a videotape of a popular TV program. What insights does it give you into the life of the community? Next, you find a perfectly preserved newspaper. What new understanding do you gain of the attitudes of the present time? Then, bit by bit, you dig up a magazine or two, a popular book, an unpopular book, the recording of a radio program, and some hit records. What now is your view of this long-vanished civilization? How do these artifacts affirm or deny (or both) the opinions you formed on the basis of seeing only buildings? Write the report you will send your university about your discoveries, and your conclusions.

Now the wise anthropologist uncovers the books, magazines, and newspapers of an earlier historical period, say that of the 1920's or 1940's. How do those findings modify your earlier conclusions?

How will today's communication methods look to the people of 2276? As you explore the past, also think about the future.

Where are we going?

part

3

LOOKING FORWARD

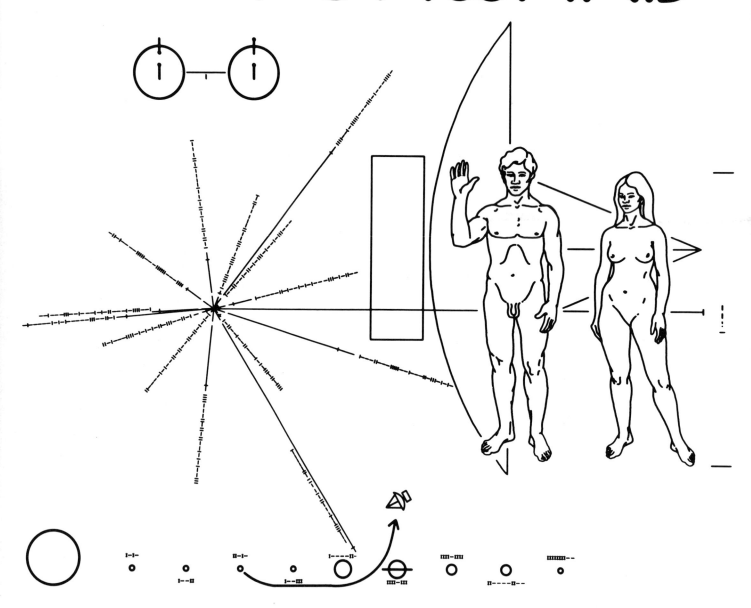

*. . . global television
could be the greatest
force yet discovered for
breaking down the
linguistic barriers that
prevent communication
between men.*

Since the Declaration of Independence, the fledgling United States has mushroomed into the greatest, wealthiest industrial and technological power in the world. Its people enjoy the highest standard of living of any society anywhere.

This phenomenal growth might not have been possible without the help of free-flowing propaganda techniques used in American mass media. The media have carried persuasive messages about industrial products, policies, and politics to millions throughout America. Propaganda for commercial or other less crass reasons has pushed America from a tiny Tom Thumb former colony into an international giant. It has supplied Americans with many of their values and has bolstered the American way of life.

But what of the future? American technology is advancing at a gigantic pace. Our present way of life may soon be obsolete. What will life in America be like when your sons and daughters are your age? What sort of propaganda

will be used to further and maintain the America of tomorrow?

Turn these pages with us and explore what some writers project as they think about the future. Then let your

imagination flow, and dream about the uses and potential of the propaganda of the late twentieth and early twenty-first centuries. What part will it play in your life and the lives of Americans yet unborn?

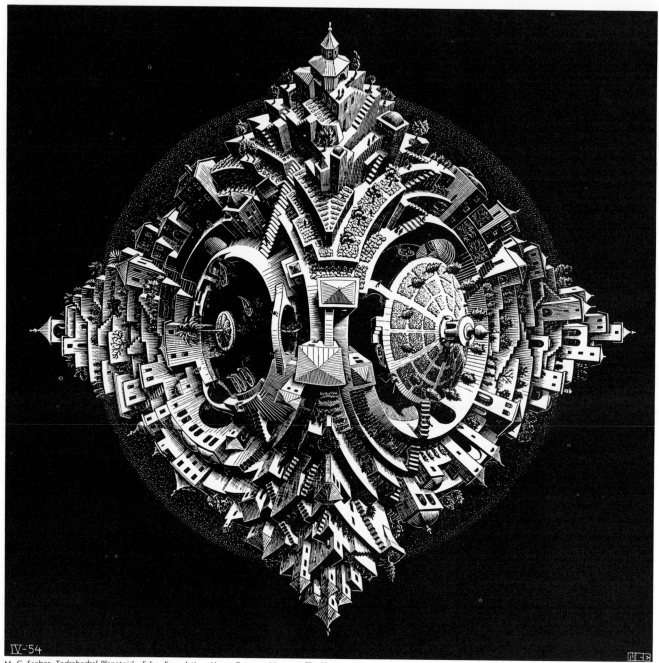

IV-54

M. C. Escher, *Tedrahedral Planetoid*—Esher Foundation, Haags Gameent Museum, The Hague.

When I dipt into the future far as human eye could see;

Saw the Vision of the world, and all the wonder that would be.-

Alfred Tennyson

Yesterday's writers peer into the future . . .

Many novelists have predicted the future. And, being writers, most have been concerned about the ways language will be used in the future, especially for propaganda and maintaining the new social order.

Here are a few worlds of tomorrow, written at various times in the past. As you read each one, consider how persuasive it is—that is, the extent to which you believe it is accurate. Consider why you do or do not believe the prophecy will come true.

In 1888 Edward Belamy wrote a novel about a man who falls asleep in 1887 and awakens in the year 2000. The main character of *Looking Backward* is toured through a vastly changed Boston by Edith Leete. Here is what happens when they go shopping:

FROM LOOKING BACKWARD

"Where is the clerk?" I asked, for there was no one behind the counter, and no one seemed coming to attend to the customer.

"I have no need of the clerk yet," said Edith. "I have not made my selection."

"It was the principal business of clerks to help people to make their selections in my day," I replied.

"What! To tell people what they wanted?"

"Yes. And oftener to induce them to buy what they didn't want."

"But did not ladies find that very impertinent?" Edith asked, wonderingly. "What concern could it possibly be to the clerks whether people bought or not?"

"It was their sole concern," I answered. "They were hired for the purpose of getting rid of the goods, and were expected to do their utmost, short of the use of force, to compass that end."

"Ah, yes! How stupid I am to forget!" said Edith. "The storekeeper and his clerks depended for their livelihood on selling the goods in your day. Of course that is all different now. The goods are the nation's. They are here for those who want them, and it is the business of the clerks to wait on people and take their orders; but it is not the interest of the clerk or the

> *The temptation to deceive the customer—or let him deceive himself—was well-nigh overwhelming.*

nation to dispose of a yard or a pound of anything to anybody who does not want it." She smiled as she added, "How exceedingly odd it must have seemed to have clerks trying to induce one to take what one did not want, or was doubtful about!"

"But even a twentieth-century clerk might make himself useful in giving you information about the goods, though he did not tease you to buy them," I suggested.

"No," said Edith, "that is not the business of the clerk. These printed cards, for which the government authorities are responsible, give us all the information we can possibly need."

I saw then that there was fastened to each sample a card containing in succinct form a complete statement of the make and materials of the goods and all its qualities, as well as price, leaving absolutely no point to hang a question on.

"The clerk has, then, nothing to say about the goods he sells?" I said.

"Nothing at all. It is not necessary that he should know or profess to know anything about them. Courtesy and accuracy in taking orders are all that are required of him."

"What a prodigious amount of lying that simple arrangement saves!" I ejaculated.

"Do you mean that all the clerks misrepresented their goods in your day?" Edith asked.

"God forbid that I should say so!" I replied. "For there were many who did not, and they were entitled to especial credit, for when one's livelihood and that of his wife and babies depended on the amount of goods he could dispose of, the temptation to deceive the customer—or let him deceive himself—was well-nigh overwhelming."

As we approach the year 2000, does the experience of shopping approach Edith's? Write a dialogue in which you explain to your descendant who will live 113 years from today what convinces you to choose some goods over others.

159

". . . If you have newspapers at all, they must, I fancy, be published by the government at the public expense, with government editors, reflecting government opinions. Now, if your system is so perfect that there is never anything to criticize in the conduct of affairs, this arrangement may answer. Otherwise I should think the lack of an independent unofficial medium for the expression of public opinion would have most unfortunate results. Confess, Doctor Leete, that a free newspaper press, with all that it implies, was a redeeming incident of the old system when capital was in private hands, and that you have to set off the loss of that against your gains in other respects."

"I am afraid I can't give you even that consolation," replied Doctor Leete, laughing. "In the first place, Mr. West, the newspaper press is by no means the only or, as we look at it, the best vehicle for serious criticism of public affairs. To us, the judgments of your newspapers on such themes seem generally to have been crude and flippant, as well as deeply tinctured with prejudice and bitterness. Insofar as they may be taken as expressing public opinion, they give an unfavorable impression of the popular intelligence, while so far as they may have formed public opinion, the nation was not to be felicitated. Nowadays, when a citizen desires to make a serious impression upon the public mind as to any aspect of public affairs, he comes out with a book or pamphlet, published as other books are. But this is not because we lack newspapers and magazines, or that they lack the most absolute freedom. The newspaper press is organized so as to be a more perfect expression of public opinion than it possibly could be in your day, when private capital controlled and managed it primarily as a moneymaking business, and secondarily only as a mouthpiece for the people."

"But," said I, "if the government prints the papers at the public expense, how can it fail to control their policy? Who appoints the editors, if not the government?"

"The government does not pay the expense of the papers, nor appoint their editors, nor in any way exert the slightest influence on their policy," replied Doctor Leete. "The people who take the paper pay the expense of its publication, choose its editor, and

remove him when unsatisfactory. You will scarcely say, I think, that such a newspaper press is not a free organ of popular opinion.''

Assume that you are one of the editors of such a newspaper in the year 2000. Write a description of your job, and mention its advantages and disadvantages.

Here's another nineteenth-century description of the future.

FROM WHEN THE SLEEPER WAKES

Life and property, indeed, were secure from violence almost all over the world, zymotic disease, bacterial diseases of all sorts had practically vanished, everyone had a sufficiency of food and clothing, was warmed in the city ways and sheltered from the weather—so much the most mechanical progress of science and the physical organisation of society had accomplished. But the crowd, he was already beginning to discover, was a crowd still, helpless in the hands of demagogue and organiser, individually cowardly, individually swayed by appetite, collectively incalculable.

H. G. Wells

With so much security in that world, what appeals might a demagogue make? Write a pamphlet such a person would distribute to the crowd.

In his novel *1984*, written in 1948, George Orwell says that language controls thought. The tyrannical future government (Ingsoc) of 1984 creates language called Newspeak, designed to prevent communication among people who oppose the dictatorship. It is supposed to prevent even *thinking* about opposition (thoughtcrime). Orwell's explanation of this process is presented in a conversation between Winston Smith, the main character of the novel, and Syme, one of the editors of the Newspeak dictionary:

FROM 1984

"How is the dictionary getting on?" said Winston, raising his voice to overcome the noise.

"Slowly," said Syme. "I'm on the adjectives. It's fascinating."

He had brightened up immediately at the mention of Newspeak.

"The Eleventh Edition is the definitive edition," he said. "We're gitting the language into its final shape—the shape it's going to have when nobody speaks anything else. When we've finished with it, people like you will have to learn it all over again. You think, I dare say, that our chief job is inventing new words. But not a bit of it! We're destroying words—scores of them, hundreds of them, every day. We're cutting the language down to the bone. The Eleventh Edition won't contain a single word that will become obsolete before the year 2050."

"It's a beautiful thing, the destruction of words. Of course the great wastage is in the verbs and adjectives, but there are hundreds of nouns that can be got rid of as well. It isn't only the synonyms; there are also the antonyms. After all, what justification is there for a word which is simply the opposite of some other words? A word contains its opposite in itself. Take 'good,' for instance. If you have a word like 'good,' what need is there for a word like 'bad'? 'Ungood' will do just as well—better, because it's an exact opposite, which the other is not. Or again, if you want a stronger version of 'good,' what sense is there in having a whole string of vague useless words like 'excellent' and 'splendid' and all the rest of them? 'Plusgood' covers the meaning, or 'doubleplusgood' if you want something stronger still. Of course we use those forms already, but in the final version of Newspeak there'll be nothing else. In the end the whole notion of goodness and badness will be covered by only six words—in reality, only one word. Don't you see the beauty of that, Winston?

"Don't you see that the whole aim of Newspeak is to narrow the range of thought? In the end we shall make thoughtcrime literally impossible, because there will be no words in which to express it. Every concept that can ever be needed will be expressed by exactly *one* word, with its meaning rigidly defined and all its subsidiary meanings rubbed out and forgotten. Already, in the Eleventh Edition, we're not far from that point. But the process will still be continuing long after you and I are dead. Every year fewer and fewer words, and the range of consciousness always a little smaller. Even now, of course, there's no reason or excuse for committing thoughtcrime. It's merely a question of self-discipline, reality-control. But in the end there won't be any need even for that. The Revolution will be complete when the language is perfect. Newspeak is Ingsoc and Ingsoc is Newspeak," he added with a sort of mystical satisfaction. "Has it ever occurred to you, Winston, that by the year 2050, at the very latest, not a single human being will be alive who could understand such a conversation as we are having now?"

"By 2050—earlier, probably—all real knowledge of Oldspeak will have disappeared. The whole literature of the past will have been destroyed. Chaucer, Shakespeare, Milton, Byron—they'll exist only in Newspeak versions, not merely changed into something different, but actually changed into something contradictory of what they used to be. Even the literature of the Party will change. Even the slogans will change. How could you have a slogan like 'freedom is slavery' when the concept of freedom has been abolished? The whole climate of thought will be different. In fact there will *be* no thought, as we understand it now. Orthodoxy means not thinking—not needing to think. Orthodoxy is unconsciousness."

Do you agree with Orwell's idea that language determines thought? What evidence can you present? We are now much closer to the year 1984 than Orwell was—do you think his prophecy is coming true?

 Write a single sentence on a current political issue; make it as unambiguous and free of varying interpretations as you possibly can.

Then pass it to several of your classmates. Have each person write down on a separate sheet of paper exactly what he understands your sentence to mean. Collect all the papers and compare them for accuracy.

On the basis of this experience, write an essay on the extent to which misinterpretation can be avoided.

Orthodoxy is unconsciousness.

Aldous Huxley's novel *Brave New World,* published in 1932, projects a world far into the future. In this excerpt, the Director of Hatcheries and Conditioning explains ''hypnopaedia'' to his students.

Today we actually do have sleep-teaching. Investigate its effectiveness, and write a brief report on it for your class. Does your research indicate that it works the way Huxley says it would?

164

Marie Marcks

FROM BRAVE NEW WORLD

"The principle of sleep-teaching, or hypnopaedia, had been discovered." The D.H.C. made an impressive pause.

"These early experimenters," The D.H.C. was saying, "were on the wrong track. They thought that hypnopaedia could be made an instrument of intellectual education . . ."

". . . You can't learn a science unless you know what it's all about.

"Whereas, if they'd only started on *moral* education . . ."

". . . Moral education, which ought never, in any circumstances, to be rational."

". . . wordless conditioning is crude and wholesale; cannot bring home the finer distinctions, cannot inculcate the more complex courses of behaviour. For that there must be words, but words without reason. In brief, hypnopaedia.

"The greatest moralizing and socializing force of all time."

Not so much like drops of water, though water, it is true, can wear holes in the hardest granite; rather, drops of liquid sealing-wax, drops that adhere, incrust, incorporate themselves with what they fall on, till finally the rock is all one scarlet blob.

"Till at last the child's mind *is* these suggestions, and the sum of the suggestions *is* the child's mind. And not the child's mind only. The adult's mind too—all his life long. The mind that judges and desires and decides —made up of these suggestions. But all these suggestions are *our* suggestions!" The Director almost shouted in his triumph. "Suggestions from the State."

Jack London, a dedicated Socialist, wrote *The Iron Heel* in 1907 to proselytize for his political belief. In this novel he portrays a terrifying future for the United States, a time when an all-enveloping capitalistic corporate state oppresses the American people. All workers are cruelly exploited for the benefit of the ruling "oligarchs." Here London explains how art will function in the Oligarchy. Consider whether there are any signs in present-day America that London's prediction is coming true.

FROM
THE IRON HEEL

"But if the Oligarchy persists," I asked him that evening, "what will become of the great surpluses that will fall to its share every year?"

"The surpluses will have to be expended somehow," he answered; "and trust the oligarchs to find a way. Magnificent roads will be built. There will be great achievements in science, and especially in art. When the oligarchs have completely mastered the people, they will have time to spare for other things. They will become worshippers of beauty. They will become art lovers. And under their direction, and generously rewarded, will toil the artists. The result will be great art; for no longer, as up to yesterday, will the artists pander to the bourgeois taste of the middle class. It will be great art, I tell you, and wonder cities will arise that will make tawdry and cheap the cities of old time. And in these cities will the oligarchs dwell and worship beauty.

"Thus will the surplus be constantly expended while labor does the work. The building of these great works and cities will give a starvation ration to millions of common laborers, for the enormous bulk of the surplus will compel an equally enormous expenditure, and the oligarchs will build for a thousand years—aye, for ten thousand years. They will build as the Egyptians and the Babylonians never dreamed of building; and when the oligarchs have passed away, their great roads and their wonder cities will remain for the brotherhood of labor to tread upon and dwell within.

"These things the oligarchs will do because they cannot help doing them. These great works will be the form their expenditure of the surplus will take, and in the same way that the ruling classes of Egypt of long ago expended the surplus they robbed from the people by the building of temples and pyramids. Under the oligarchs will flourish, not a priest class, but an artist class. And in place of the merchant class of bourgeoisie will be the labor castes. And beneath will be the abyss, wherein will fester and starve and rot, and ever renew itself, the common people, the great bulk of the population."

In the course of the novel, a highly respected bishop comes to realize the destructiveness of the Establishment. He preaches against it, but his talk is forcibly stopped by oligarchs who claim that he is ill and doesn't know what he is saying. Some of his supporters believe that the bishop's message will be relayed, anyway, when the newspapers report his statement. Here is the reply of the hero of the novel:

"Not a word that he uttered will see print. You have forgotten the editors. They draw their salaries for the policy they maintain. Their policy is to print nothing that is a vital menace to the established. The Bishop's utterance was a violent assault upon the established morality. It was heresy. They led him from the platform to prevent him from uttering more heresy. The newspapers will purge his heresy in the oblivion of silence. The press of the United States? It is a parasitic growth that fattens on the capitalist class. Its function is to serve the established by moulding public opinion, and right well it serves it."

As London tells it, a Nazi-like atmosphere develops which he prophetically labels "the iron heel." He severely criticizes the U.S. press for facilitating this development, either by remaining silent or by distorting reality.

All was quiet as we entered Chicago. It was evident nothing had happened yet. In the suburbs the morning papers came on board the train. There was nothing in them, and yet there was much in them for those skilled in reading between the lines that it was intended the ordinary reader should read into the text. The fine hand of the Iron Heel was apparent in every column. Glimmerings of weakness in the armor of the Oligarchy were given. Of course, there was nothing definite. It was intended that the reader should feel his way to these glimmerings. It was cleverly done. As fiction, these morning papers of October 27th were masterpieces.

Write two paragraphs similar to London's in which you either refute or support his position.

In *Erewhon*, a land where everything is as backward as its name, education has aims that are opposite to ours. Or are they?

Samuel Butler's novel was published in 1872 in England. Were the Erewhon Professors' teachings on progress the opposite of those of the British Victorians'? Read something about their activities and write a proper Victorian response to the Professors.

FROM EREWHON

"It is not our business," he said, "to help students to think for themselves. Surely this is the very last thing which one who wishes them well should encourage them to do. Our duty is to ensure that they shall think as we do, or at any rate, as we hold it expedient to say we do."

I told them of Homer's noble line to the effect that a man should strive ever to be foremost and in all things to outvie his peers; but they said that no wonder the countries in which such a detestable maxim was held in admiration were always flying at one another's throats.

"Why," asked one Professor, "should a man want to be better than his neighbors? Let him be thankful if he is no worse."

"We like progress," he said, "but it must commend itself to the common sense of the people. If a man gets to know more than his neighbors he should keep his knowledge to himself till he has sounded them, and seen whether they agree, or are likely to agree with him. He said it was as immoral to be too far in front of one's own age, as to lag too far behind it. If a man can carry his neighbors with him, he may say what he likes; but if not, what insult can be more gratuitous than the telling them what they do not want to know? A man should remember that intellectual over-indulgence is one of the most insidious and disgraceful forms that excess can take."

. . . think as we do or, at any rate, as we hold it expedient to say we do.

Today's writers view tomorrow . . .

Ray Bradbury's prediction of the future world, in his novel *Fahrenheit 451*, focuses on a man named Montag, a fireman. In that time, a fireman's job consists not of stopping fires, but of starting them— whenever an alarm comes in that books are present anywhere, the firemen rush out and burn them. In this section, Fire Chief Beatty tells Montag and his wife, Mildred, the causes and needs for the work he does.

FROM FAHRENHEIT 451

"When did it all start, you ask, this job of ours, how did it come about, where, when? Well, I'd say it really got started around about a thing called the Civil War. Even though our rule book claims it was founded earlier. The fact is we didn't get along well until photography came into its own. Then—motion pictures in the early Twentieth Century. Radio. Television. Things began to have *mass*."

Montag sat in bed, not moving.

"And because they had mass, they became simpler," said Beatty. "Once, books appealed to a few people, here, there, everywhere. They could afford to be different. The world was roomy. But then the world got full of eyes and elbows and mouths. Double, triple, quadruple population. Films and radios, magazines, books leveled down to a sort of paste pudding norm, do you follow me?"

"I think so."

Beatty peered at the smoke pattern he had put out on the air. "Picture it. Nineteenth-century man with his horses, dogs, carts, slow motion. Then, in the

continued

Twentieth Century, speed up your camera. Books cut shorter. Condensations. Digests. Tabloids. Everything boils down to the gag, the snap ending."

"Snap ending," Mildred nodded.

"Classics cut to fit fifteen-minute radio shows, then cut again to fill two-minute book column, winding up at last as a ten- or twelve-line dictionary resume. I exaggerate, of course. The dictionaries were for reference. But many were those whose sole knowledge of *Hamlet* (you know the title certainly, Montag; it is probably only a faint rumor of a title to you, Mrs. Montag), whose sole knowledge, as I say, of *Hamlet* was a one-page digest in a book that claimed: *now at last you can read all the classics; keep up with your neighbors.* Do you see? Out of the nursery into the college and back to the nursery; there's your intellectual pattern for the past five centuries or more."

"Speed up the film, Montag, quick. *Click, Pic, Look, Eye, Now, Flick, Here, There, Swift, Pace, Up, Down, In, Out, Why, How, Who, What, Where, Eh? Uh! Bang! Smack! Wallop, Bing, Bong, Boom!* Digest-digests, digest-digest-digests. Politics? One column, two sentences, a headline! Then, in mid-air, all vanishes! Whirl man's mind around about so fast under the pumping hands of publishers, exploiters, broadcasters that the centrifuge flings off all unnecessary, time-wasting thought!"

"School is shortened, discipline relaxed, philosophies, histories, languages dropped, English and spelling gradually neglected, finally almost completely ignored. Life is immediate, the job counts, pleasure lies all about after work. Why learn anything save pressing buttons, pulling switches, fitting nuts and bolts?"

"Empty the theaters save for clowns and furnish the rooms with glass walls and pretty colors running up and down the walls like confetti or blood or sherry or sauterne. You like baseball, don't you, Montag?"

"Baseball's a fine game."

"Billiards, pool? Football?"

"Fine games, all of them."

"More sports for everyone, group spirit, fun, and you don't have to think, eh? Organize and organize and super organize super-super sports. More cartoons in books. More pictures. The mind drinks less and

continued

Print nothing that is a vital menace to the established.

170

Moral education ought never, in any circumstances, be rational.

less. Impatience. Highways full of crowds going somewhere, somewhere, somewhere, nowhere. The gasoline refugee. Towns turn into motels, people in nomadic surges from place to place, following the moon tides, living tonight in the room where you slept this noon and I the night before."

"A book is a loaded gun in the house next door. Burn it. Take the shot from the weapon. Breach man's mind. Who knows who might be the target of the well-read man? Me? I won't stomach them for a minute.

"If you don't want a man unhappy politically, don't give him two sides to a question to worry him; give him one. Better yet, give him none. Let him forget there is such a thing as war. If the government is inefficient, top-heavy, and tax-mad, better it be all those than that people worry over it. Peace, Montag. Give the people contests they win by remembering the words to more popular songs or the names of state capitals or how much corn Iowa grew last year. Cram them full of noncombustible data, chock them so damned full of 'facts' they feel stuffed, but absolutely 'brilliant' with information. Then they'll feel they're thinking, they'll get a *sense* of motion without moving. And they'll be happy, because facts of that sort don't change. Don't give them any slippery stuff like philosophy or sociology to tie things up with. That way lies melancholy."

What evidence do you see in the present-day world that supports the ideas Bradbury presents here? What evidence do you see that denies his views. Make a list of each. Then write a paragraph stating which one you personally find most persuasive.

A book is a loaded gun in the house next door.

PARCHMENT
BRAND   No. 3 - 12 lines   Printed in U.S.A.

Belwin Inc.
New York, U.S.A.

A FEMINIST SEES THE FUTURE

Let's look to the year 2000 and consider just the world of work, the world of the home, and the world of education. Because woman's experience is now changing more and faster than man's, if we look at the direction of that change, I believe we will be able to predict the direction of the total change in our society. This is not to say that women are smarter or more perceptive than men. But women are pointing the way because their new attitudes are a response to a changed reality in society and in economics.

What will happen if women really do achieve their goals? I see a most attractive future in that: a world in which both men and women enter a job because it appeals to them, rather than because that is what is expected of a man, or that is all that is available to a woman.

Perhaps then, by the year 2000, we will see acceptance of the idea of training each person according to his individual interests and abilities. We will see the rejection of the idea of setting certain occupations aside for men only, preferably white Protestant men.

What results can we expect from these new attitudes? One thing that might happen is that black and white and red and brown and yellow women and men will enter the medical schools, the dental schools, the law schools, the engineering schools, and all the others that have been private reserves. The presence of this mixture will enrich the service professions and enable them to extend and broaden their services in ways that have not been possible until now.

With freedom from stereotyped thinking and with a feeling of

174

equality between husband and wife, the household of the future should be a more peaceable place. But how will the housekeeping functions be accomplished?

Perhaps the wife will also be the housewife. Feminists have never rejected this role for women. They have rejected only forcing every woman into the role whether she likes it or not. Any woman who chooses to be a housewife will, of course, be free to do so. And like other workers, she will be given compensation for the job and a pension when she retires.

Or perhaps the husband would choose to be the household manager. When jobs are no longer stereotyped by sex, he will feel free to do so if he prefers.

Perhaps husband and wife do the housework jointly. That is the most likely pattern to evolve, and one that we already see on a fairly widespread basis. Perhaps what will occur is that professional housekeeping firms will provide what B. F. Skinner calls "the industrialization of housewifery." It is unlikely that personal housekeeping will remain a central purpose of anybody's life.

Discuss this feminist point of view with your classmates.

Choose one of the issues raised in this statement and write a full argument, stating your own view of the situation.

All great truths begin as blasphemies.

George Bernard Shaw

FUTURISTIC
MEDIA

Read the following passage. Then summarize what the author is saying in a paragraph. Try not to imitate the author's style. Express yourself in your own language.

A COMMENT ON
THE FUTURE OF PROPAGANDA

. . . Clearly propaganda will be shaped in terms of the nature of future media. For example, in wall-size holographic (3-D) TV, the framed plane which previously (in our history) focused the action, begins to disappear. The concept of the "living room" will perhaps take on new meaning when we can go into it to watch the ocean spray as if one were at the beach or right in the ocean. No doubt viewers will be able to differentiate actual (natural) events from the projected versions, but the differentiation will be subtler and at the same time more incisive than it is now, without the frame to cue the viewer. It would appear, then, that wall-size TV might be an unusually effective manipulator of beliefs, since the very act of programming for such a medium (blowing up some things, cutting out others) shapes a "reality" that people can believe in because they see it. Such propaganda could very well be invisible, slipped unobtrusively into the programming (news, soap-operas) even more deliberately than it is now. When the frame is taken away, it is harder for people to differentiate media assumptions from reality: it always was the frame that allowed people to know (if they cared to) that they were perceiving propaganda. It is for this reason that present-day advertising tries to resort to techniques of subliminal cueing, and that past propagandists tried to keep propaganda as invisible as possible. Certainly, with the frame taken away, people will have even less of a chance to see that they are being shaped. Frameups occur without anyone knowing that they are being framed. . . .

Richard Watson

177

Free news by A.D. 2000

As social ownership of the press develops, more and more newspapers will be entirely managed by professional journalists. In the beginning such managers will be appointed by higher cooperative or government officials, but eventually all will be chosen by regional or national professional associations of journalists, in order to minimize political control over the press.

The rise of socialism has already eliminated most advertising in newspapers and magazines published behind the iron curtain. It will produce similar results in all other countries before 2200. Since most advertising is socially wasteful, special taxes or quotas on advertising will soon be enacted in some capitalist states and will multiply and grow thereafter. The gradual elimination of most advertising from newspapers will equally reduce the space given to publicity stories tied to advertising.

Radical changes in newspaper news and feature content are inevitable. Capitalist newspapers now play up crimes, divorces, scandals, accidents. Such stories grossly impair the administration of justice and cause an enormous amount of personal embarrassment and unhappiness. Many witnesses lie or withhold evidence in order to avoid harmful publicity. As men become more intelligent and better educated, they are sure to limit and eventually prohibit more and more stories liable to have such effects. All criminal and divorce proceedings will become secret before 2100. Even the court decisions will then be transmitted only to officials and private persons who need such information.

It is customary for readers to preserve newspapers for a few days only. Hence editors will eventually eliminate all printed matter which should be preserved more than a few days—fiction, humor, popular science, how-to-do-it stories, memoirs, etc. Such matter will be printed in books, which can be more easily preserved, passed on to others, and made available in libraries. When advertising has been curtailed by 90 percent, and all newspapers have become monopolies, their editors will have little reason to try to build circulation by including non-news items in papers. And it is wasteful to print items which ought to be preserved, in daily papers which are not preserved. Separate publication of feature material will permit readers to buy only the printed matter they want.

The gradual elimination of advertising, crime and scandal stories, comics, fiction, and other non-news items will make United States newspapers thinner and thinner. In 1960 big-city papers averaged over 50 pages an issue; by 2200 this figure will fall below 12.

The marginal cost of printing and delivering such newspapers will be small. Moreover, it will be socially desirable to encourage universal reading of them. Hence they will become free goods, financed entirely by taxation, before A.D. 2200.

Burnham Putnam Beckwith

 Write some headlines and news items for a newspaper of the future.

From *The Next 500 Years: Scientific Predictions of Major Social Trends* by Burnham P. Beckwith. © 1967 by Burnham Putnam Beckwith. Reprinted by permission of Exposition Press, Inc., Jericho, N.Y. 11753.

THERE'S BETTER THINGS

Kind friends I want to warn you
Because I love us all,
No doubt you read your papers,
But the half can never be told.
Politicians will try and fool you, and get you to agree
To blow this world to glory and end humanity.

But there's better things to do—than blow this world in two
You could live into your old age, and your kids be normal too.
There's better things for you—that all on earth must do
Gotta pledge your feet on the road to peace and
see your journey through.
Now some folks think that danger
Can't reach this peaceful shore
They must see planes and soldiers
Before they call it war.
Kind friends I will remind you
The atom's very small
It can blow you all to glory
And you can't see it at all.

CHORUS:
Now some folks they are holy
In the Bible it is told
That Judgment comes tomorrow
So today pray for your soul.
But that is not sufficient
Tomorrow is today
They'll blow you all to glory
While you just sit and pray.

Peggy Seeger

179

Write your own title for this passage . . .

_____

_____

_____

Now I would like to say a word about communications. The revolution in communications that has already taken place is still not fully understood. One way of appreciating it is to do a kind of communciations strip tease. I would like you to abolish in your minds TV, then radio, then telephones, then the postal service, then the newspapers. In other words, to revert to the Middle Ages, and in fact to the state of affairs most of mankind has known for most of its history—and which much of mankind still knows. In such a situation we should feel deaf and blind, like prisoners in solitary confinement.
Well, we'll appear this way to our grandchildren. Don't forget that a generation has already grown up that never knew a world without TV. One communications revolution has taken place in our lifetime. The next revolution, perhaps the final one, will be the result of satellites and microelectronics, which will enable us to do literally anything we want to in the field of communications and information transfer—including, ultimately, not only sound and vision but _all_ sense impressions.

I am particularly interested in TV broadcasting from satellites _directly into the home_, bypassing today's ground stations—a proposal I first described twenty-two years ago. This will mean the abolition of all present geographical restrictions to TV; via satellites, any country can broadcast to any other. Direct-broadcast TV will be possible within five years and may be most important to undeveloped countries that have no ground stations, and now may never require any. Africa, China, and South America could be opened up by direct TV broadcast, and whole populations brought into the modern world. I believe that communications satellites may bring about the long-overdue end of the Stone Age.

They will certainly lead to a global telephone system and end long-distance calls—for _all_ calls will be "local"! There will be the same flat rate everywhere; possibly we may not even pay for calls but will merely rent the equipment for unlimited use.

Newspapers will, I think, receive their final body blow from these new communications techniques. I take a dim view of staggering home every Sunday with five pounds of wood pulp on my arm, when what I really want is information, not wastepaper. How I look forward to the day when I can press a button and get any type of news, editorials, book and theater reviews, etc., merely by dialing the right channel. The print will flash on the screen, and if I want "hard copy" to file or read elsewhere, another button will conjure forth a printed sheet containing _only_ what I need.

Moreover, not only today's but _any_ newspaper ever published will be available. Some sort of TV-like console, connected to a central electronic library, could make available any information ever printed in any form.

Arthur C. Clarke

Write an essay exploring the effect you think Arthur Clarke's view of tomorrow's communication will have on advertising of the future.

Satellites and sales . . .

A fairly modest satellite, which we can build today, could provide a thousand voice channels across the Atlantic, or alternatively a single television circuit. Looking only a decade or two into the future, one can foresee the time when a network of advanced satellites will bring all points on the Earth into close contact so far as telephony is concerned. It will be as quick and easy to call Australia from Greenland, or South America from China, as it is now to put through a local call. Indeed, by the end of this century all terrestrial calls may be local calls and may be billed at a flat standard rate.

This may have as great an effect on business and social life as the invention of the telephone itself. Just how great that was, we of today have forgotten; perhaps we can remind ourselves by imagining that the telephone was suddenly abolished and we had to conduct all business face to face or else by correspondence carried by stagecoach and sailing ship. To our grandchildren we will still seem in that primitive level of development, and our present patterns of daily commuting a fantastic nightmare. For ask yourself how much traveling you would really have to do if you had an office in your own home and wide-screen, full-color television through which you could be in face-to-face contact with anyone on Earth. A good nine-tenths of the traveling

continued

that now takes place could be avoided with better communications.

There can be no doubt that satellites will have an especially great effect on the transmission of written and printed information. One idea that has been discussed at some length is the Orbital Post Office, which may make most air mail obsolete in a decade or so. A single satellite, using modern facsimile equipment, could easily handle the whole of today's trans-atlantic correspondence. Eventually, letters should never take more than a few minutes to be delivered to any point on the Earth, and one can even visualize the time when all correspondence is sent by direct person-to-person facsimile circuits. When that time comes, the post office will cease to handle letters, except where the originals are required, and will concern itself only with parcels.

Wonder cities will arise.

Another development that will have the most far-reaching consequences is the Orbital Newspaper; this is inevitable once the idea gets around that what most people need is information, not wood pulp. Half a century from now, newspapers as we know them may not exist, except as trains of electronic impulses. When you wish to read the *New York Times*, you will dial the appropriate number on your channel selector, just as today you

182

call a party on the telephone. The front page would then appear on your high-definition screen, at least as sharp and clear as on a microfilm reader; it would remain there until you pressed a button, when it would be replaced by page two, and so on.

Of course, the entire format would be completely redesigned for the new medium; perhaps there would be separate channels for editorials, book reviews, business, news, classified advertising, etc. If you needed a permanent record (and just how often do you save your daily paper?), that could easily be arranged by an attachment like a Polaroid camera or one of the high speed copying devices now found in all modern offices.

Not only the local paper but all the papers of all countries could be viewed in this way, merely by dialing the right number—and back issues, too, since this would require nothing more than appropriate extra coding.

This leads us directly into the enormous and exciting field of information storage and retrieval, which is one of the basic problems of our culture. It is now possible to store any written material or any illustration in electronic form —as, for example, is done every day on video tape. One can thus envisage a Central Library or Memory Bank, which would be a permanent part of the world communications network. Readers and scholars could call for any document, from the Declaration of Independence to the current best

seller and see it flashed on their screens.

The Electronic Library is bound to come; its development is being forced by the rising flood of printed matter. Recently, a storage device was announced that could contain everything ever written or printed on stone, paper or papyrus during the last ten thousand years inside a six-foot cube. The problem of encoding and indexing all the world's literature in electronic form so that any part of it can be retrieved and played back is a staggering one, but it has to be solved before our libraries collapse under the weight of their books. And when it is solved, any man on Earth who knows how to dial the right numbers will have immediate access to all printed knowledge, flashed from Central Memory Bank up to the nearest satellite and down again to be displayed on the screen of his receiver. If he wishes, he will be able to store it in his own electronic library for easy reference, as we now record music or conversation on tape, although the recording medium will certainly be much more compact and convenient.

The most glamorous possibility opened up by communications satellites is the one which I originally stressed in 1945—global radio and television. This will be something quite new in the world, and we have no precedents to guide us. For the first time one nation will be able to speak directly to the people of another, and to project images into their homes,

with or without the cooperation of the other government concerned. Today's short-wave sound broadcasts are only poor and feeble things compared to those which the clear, interference-free reception from satellites will make possible.

I sometimes wonder if the enormous efforts that most large nations now expend on short-wave broadcasting are worth it, in view of the poor quality of reception. But this will change when the direct and far more efficient line-of-sight services from satellites become available. A Londoner, for example, will be able to tune into NBC or CBS or Radio Moscow as easily and clearly as to the BBC. The engineers and scientists now struggling to establish reliable satellite circuits with the aid of antennas the size of football fields will tell you that this is still years in the future, and they may be right. Nevertheless, most of us will see the day when every home will be fitted with radio and TV equipment that can tune directly to transmitters orbiting thousands of miles above the Earth, and the last barriers to free communications will be down.

These who are already glutted with entertainment and information from their local stations may be less than enthusiastic about this. However, they are a tiny minority of the human race. Most of the world does not even have radio, still less television. I would suggest, therefore, that though the first use of satellites will be to provide increased facilities be-

continued

tween already highly developed countries, their greatest political and cultural influence will be upon backward and even preliterate peoples.

For in the 1970's we will be able to put megawatt transmitters into orbit and will also have reliable battery-powered television receivers that can be mass-produced at a cost which even small African or Asian villages can afford.

Quite apart from its direct visual impact, the effect of TV will be incomparably greater than that of radio because it is so much less dependent upon language. Men can enjoy pictures even when they cannot understand the words that go with them. Moreover, the pictures may encourage them to understand those words. If it is used properly, global television could be the greatest force yet discovered for breaking down the linguistic barriers that prevent communication between men.

Nobody knows how many languages there are in the world; estimates run to as high as six thousand. But a mere seven are spoken by half the human race, and it is interesting to list the percentages. First by a substantial margin comes Mandarin, the language of 15 per cent of mankind. Then comes English, 10 per cent. After that there is a large gap, and grouped together round the 5 per cent level we find in this order: Hindustani, Spanish, Russian, German, and Japanese. But these are mother tongues, and far more people understand English than normally speak it. On

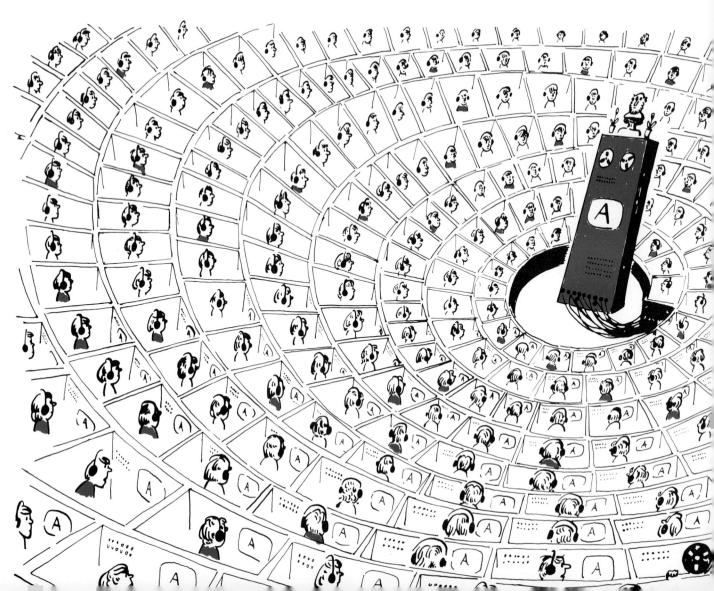

the basis of world comprehension, English undoubtedly leads all other languages.

Helpless in the hands of demagogue and organizer.

Few subjects touch upon national pride and prejudices as much as does language, yet everyone recognizes the immense value and importance of a tongue which all educated men can understand. I think that, within a lifetime, communications satellites may give us just that. Unless some synthetic language comes to the fore—which seems improbable—the choice appears to be between Mandarin, English, and, for obvious reasons, Russian, even though it is only fifth on the list and understood by less than 5 per cent of mankind. Perhaps it will be a photo finish, and our grand-children will be bi- or trilingual. I will venture no predictions, but I would stress again that it is impossible to underestimate the importance of communications satellites in this particular domain.

Television satellites will also present us, and that, soon, with acute problems in international relations. Suppose country A starts transmitting what the government of country B considers to be subversive propaganda. This is happening all the time, of course, but no one complains too bitterly

continued

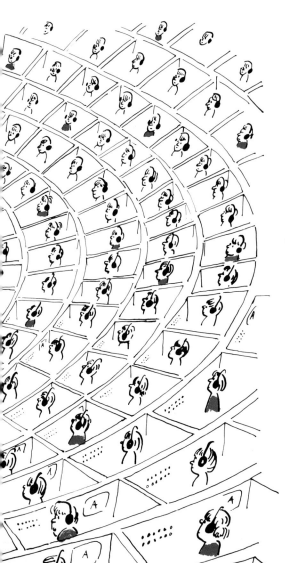

The alternatives to persuasion are either a wholly individualistic society or a completely coercive one—a society in which force has replaced persuasion. In all other forms of society it is necessary for people to secure the cooperation of other people, and this implies the use of persuasion.

Wentworth K. Brown, Sterling P. Olmsted

today because the process is relatively ineffective and is confined to radio. Just imagine, however, what Dr. Goebbels could have done with a chain of global TV stations, perhaps capable of putting down stronger signals in many countries than could be produced by the local transmitters, if any.

There would be only two ways of countering such unwanted propaganda. An aggrieved government might try to prevent the sale of receivers that could tune to the offending frequencies, or it might try jamming. Neither policy would be very effective, and jamming could only be carried out from another satellite, which would probably cause protests from the rest of the world, owing to the interference with legitimate transmissions elsewhere.

Though there are obvious dangers and possibilities of friction, on the whole I am very optimistic about this breaking down of national communications barriers, holding to the oldfashioned belief that in the long run right will prevail. I also look forward, with more than a little interest, to the impact of non-commercial television upon audiences which so far have not had much choice in the matter. Millions of Americans have never known the joys of sponsorless radio or television; they are like readers who know only books full of advertisements which they are not allowed to skip. How would reading have fared in these circumstances? And how will Madison Avenue fare, when it no longer controls the video channels? Perhaps the apocalypse of the agencies has already been described in Revelations, chapter 18: "... And the merchants of the earth shall weep and mourn ... for no man buyeth their merchandise any more: The merchandise of gold, and silver, and precious stones ... and ointments ... and wine, and oil ... and chariots ... and souls of men." This last commodity, I believe, is one expended in massive quantities by commercial television.

Arthur C. Clarke

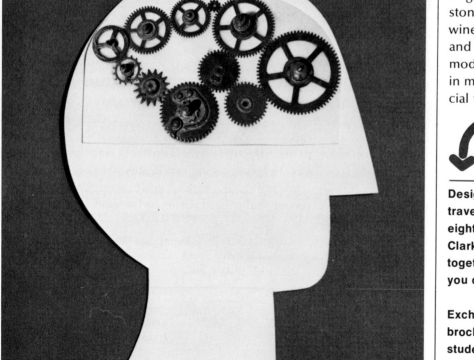

Design, write, and illustrate a travel brochure containing at least eight pages. Base it on Arthur Clarke's projections in this passage together with any imaginative ideas you can muster.

Exchange your completed brochure with those of other students. Write a critical analysis of the propaganda techniques used in some of your fellow students' projects.

Psyche-service and psych-corps . . .

Exchange your work with that of another student and criticize each other's propaganda techniques.

Before beginning the assignment, study the passage below, as well as the excerpts in this book by Arthur Clarke, Richard Watson, and Putnam Beckwith.

Imagine that you have been employed by a large "psych-corps" to advertise a super-Disneyland of the future.

Select the futuristic media most suitable and outline an advertising campaign. Then write the kind of copy you think would be appropriate.

But the great psych-corps of tomorrow will not only sell individual, discrete experiences. They will offer sequences of experiences so organized that their very juxtaposition with one another will contribute color, harmony or contrast to lives that lack these qualities. Beauty, excitement, danger or delicious sensuality will be programmed to enhance one another. By offering such experiential chains or sequences, the psych-corps (working closely, no doubt, with community mental health centers) will provide partial frameworks for those whose lives are otherwise too chaotic and unstructured. In effect, they will say: "Let us plan (part of) your life for you." In the transient, change-filled world of tomorrow, that proposition will find many eager takers.

The packaged experiences offered in the future will reach far beyond the imagination of the average consumer, filling the environment with endless novelties. Companies will vie with one another to create the most outlandish, most gratifying experiences. Indeed, some of these experiences—as in the case of topless Swedish models—will even reach beyond tomorrow's broadened boundaries of social acceptability. They may be offered to the public covertly by unlicensed, underground psych-corps. This will simply add the thrill of "illicitude" to the experience itself.

(One very old experiential industry has traditionally operated covertly: prostitution. Many other illegal activities also fit within the experience industry. For the most part, however, all these reveal a paucity of imagination and lack of technical resources that will be remedied in the future. They are trivial compared with the possibilities in a society that will, by the year 2000 or sooner, be armed with robots, advanced computers, personality-altering drugs, brain-stimulating pleasure probes, and similar technological goodies.)

The diversity of novel experiences arrayed before the consumer will be the work of experience-designers, who will be drawn from the ranks of the most creative people in the society. The working motto of this profession will be: "If you can't serve it up real, find a vicarious substitute. If you're good, the customer will never know the difference!" This implied blurring of the line between the real and the unreal will confront the society with serious problems, but it will not prevent or even slow the emergence of the "psyche-service industries" and "psych-corps." Great globe-girdling syndicates will create super-Disneylands of a variety, scale, scope, and emotional power that is hard for us to imagine.

Alvin Toffler

"If you can't serve it up real, find a vicarious substitute. If you're good, the customer will never know the difference!"

From *Future Shock*, by Alvin Toffler. Copyright © 1970 by Alvin Toffler. Reprinted by permission of Random House, Inc.

CLASSIFIED ADVERTISEMENTS

LOGIC FROM ANOTHER WORLD

AN ASTROLOGICAL APPEAL

"24Z! 25Z! Get away from that telescan! You've been sitting there for hours when you should be outside practicing your flying. Why do you think I bought you new stellajets?"

"But, MotherZ, it's astral to watch the Earthpersons. They're so funny! You can't believe the things they say."

"And MotherZ, wait till you see their graphing. Just look for a minute while I switch the telescan through some of their books. You'll laugh too."

"O, no, I'm not going to spend my millennium snooping on the Earthpersons . . . I've got space-search to do."

"Please, MotherZ, just for a moonflash."

"You'll have fun with us."

"Well, 24Z, 25Z, all right. But not for long."

"Here, listen to that speaker. It thinks it's presenting a *deductive argument*. It says that starodomes are astral links and spacemobiles are astral links, therefore space-mobiles are starodomes. What a *syllogism!*"

"Ho ho! Who would believe it?"

"The Earthpersons, that's who! We told you they're funny."

"Haven't they ever heard of the need for *evidence?*"

"What they call evidence are just *emotional appeals*—to their vanity or prejudices or sentimentality. They never give *facts*, just *opinions.*"

"24Z! Who's indulging in negative argument now? What do you mean 'never give facts'?"

"Well . . . the majority of the time, they give opinions as though they were facts."

"That's better."

"I'm glad we learn *logic*—how to present a valid argument and sound evidence—at the same time we learn articulation. That prevents all the confusion they have on Earth."

"Listen to this now—listen, they're singing, 'The skies are not cloudy all day.' Did you ever hear such *ambiguity?*"

"Ho ho ho—you have to be narking!"

"Now, pay attention to this one. It's talking about us. It says we live on an Astrak, engage in selfmobilization, and do not appear on Earthscans; therefore, we're not intelligent beings."

"Incredible! I'll bet it calls that an *inductive argument.*"

"It just doesn't know the *rules of inference.*"

"O, those poor persons. If only they could express themselves clearly and *persuade* one another on the basis of a *rational* syllogism instead of indulging in all those logical fallacies, their lives would be so much happier. They would really know what they're doing— and why. They'd be in control of their own destiny."

"Say! I've got an idea—let's beam them some Astrologic."

"Good idea, 25Z. But how will we we persuade them to use it?"

"Well . . ."

How do you think this discussion might proceed?

A PROPAGANDA PROPOSAL FROM OUTER SPACE

The farmyard was in a furore. The unbelievable had arrived. The spaceship, with its bright yellow cone-shaped structure, was standing menacingly by the side of the duck pond. It must have arrived in the night. It had no windows that anyone could see, but here and there were small, raised, conical projections. Out of one of these, beams of vivid green light darted at any creature that approached.

The animals and birds were terrified, yet they could not overcome their curiosity. Where had this strange object come from? Who was inside it? What did they look like? What would these creatures do? Why were they here? Was it the beginning of an invasion that would destroy Earth? Had other spaceships like this one landed? Perhaps hundreds or thousands of them? All these questions coursed through their uneasy minds.

Mother Goose was almost hysterical. "They'll destroy us all," she screamed. "Proper Gander, you've got to do something."

Proper Gander wanted to show how controlled and masculine he was. He tried hard not to betray his emotions. "I am thinking about what I can do," he replied. "At the moment, I think discretion is the better part of valor. The State Police, even the National Guard, will be called out and they will do something. It's out of control. What can we, a group of animals, do? What can our farmer do? He has a shotgun, I know, but he'd be a fool to use it. I've heard about these spaceships. They are made of material which deflects bullets and, in turn, they have powerful rays which can burn up everything in sight. I'm just as terrified as you are, and I'd do something If I knew what to do, but I feel so helpless."

At that moment, Tom Turkey rushed up to them, quivering with fright. "Come," he said, "there's —there's some—something happening."

The birds joined a group of other animals that were huddled together. There was indeed something happening. Out of one of the small projections came a thick, black substance like molten tar or asphalt. It formed a gooey puddle on the ground.

Everybody watched, mesmerized, as the black substance oozed out. As they watched, they huddled closer together, gaining some comfort from the nearness of their fellows.

Then the tarlike substance began to evaporate and form into a circular, opaque screen, and on the screen a message began to appear in clear, yellow letters. Soon the screen was about ten feet in diameter, and the message was clearly visible.

"Do not be afraid," it read. "We have not come here to harm you. We want to help you. We will not come out of our Planetship because we have so little time and many more errands to accomplish. You cannot enter our ship because you would be killed by the atmospheric conditions in it. Read our message and believe it. We have tried to communicate with human beings, but they do not appear to believe in UFOs, as they call us. Human beings suspect us of aggressive intentions. They think we are warlike because they are. They believe that we wish to conquer and have power over

From the Herblock Gallery (Simon & Schuster, 1968).

others because that is the way they think. Only humans on Planet Earth are makers of war upon their kind for the purpose of power, but perhaps they can be persuaded that this is not the law of the universe. We have the technological power to make slaves of the human race if we wished to, but we do not wish to control them, only to cooperate with them. Since we cannot reach people because of their disbelief in us, we are talking to the other Earth creatures.

"Our close observations over a long period of time have shown us dramatically that human society is wallowing in a quagmire of difficult problems, and that many of these problems are caused by the misuse of language.

"Human language is complex and one of the miracles of Planet Earth. In one sense, it separates people from other creatures. The language of people is highly symbolic in nature and has enabled them to build upon the past and to create modern, advanced ways of living. Animals have not been able to accomplish this yet.

"Great civilizations, with their complex technological knowledge, are tottering and may fall. For many people, the future looks hopeless, dehumanizing, and full of despair. A major reason for this is that human beings are misusing their language to such an extent that people have only the deepest cynicism for the statements of their political leaders, industrial leaders, and leaders at almost every level.

"Hour after hour, day after day, month in and year out, the mass media bombard people with a barrage of doublespeak—misuse of language—in the form of illogical arguments, emotional appeals, false claims, testimonials, lying statistics, gobbledygook, exaggeration, jargon, and other forms of misrepresentation.

"Doublespeak has invaded all levels of sophisticated society. It has become a form of established and accepted behavior. But it should be seen as a disease which must be combatted and eliminated if the future of the human race is to become worth facing. Word-truth will do away with frustration, hate, prejudice, and anger, and will replace unhappiness with trust.

"On our Planet, we banned doublespeak a long time ago. It is a capital offense to use it. We allow persuasion only as a force for the good. As a result, we have no sense of distrust in our society. Since there is no such thing as misrepresentation, an individual's word is as good as his bond.

"We urge you to persuade people to work for the abolition of doublespeak. They have got to stop cheating and manipulating one another with words if they sincerely want to begin curing some of their social ills.

"This ends our message to you now. We must move on to another area and another group of animals. Soon we will be back to hear of your progress."

As the animals watched, the screen vanished. A few moments later, the spaceship lifted off the ground and rose up through the clouds to disappear.

"I really can't believe what I've just seen," said Mother Goose.

"Well, there are plenty of witnesses," said Proper Gander, "but it sounds like a lot of doublespeak to me, and I'm cynical about it."

Mother Goose looked at him, her eyes burning with intensity. "Has it occurred to you that the creatures in the spaceship were bringing us a message with persuasion for the good instead of using coercion, which they certainly could employ? Yes, it was propaganda, but not all propaganda is negative or self-seeking. They are using persuasion for very positive reasons. They want to help people cure their own disease. I hear what they have to say. I want to believe them. I want to help them achieve what they suggest. What I read today gives me tremendous hope and faith in the future because, with their cooperation, we can teach human beings some ways to benefit all of us on Earth. I look forward to the time when they will return."

"But how are we going to reach people?" asked Proper Gander, perplexed.

"Propaganda, of course," said Mother Goose with a knowing smile.

Compose an essay in which you explore examples of propaganda that you feel are used for non-mercenary, sincere, and honest purposes.

PROJECTS AND PROJECTIONS

Thinking ahead . . .

→ To help you think beyond this book, here are some exercises that can constitute final projects.

1

When you started this book, you may have believed that the propaganda you experienced had little impact on you and did not affect your personal life. After exploring this book, do you still believe that? Work your reply into a paragraph or two.

2

Does it strike you as odd that so much advertising in this country seems to be aimed at a low level of intelligence? Surely, it must be worthwhile to the advertisers to keep things this way or they would not waste their money. How can it be that this kind of situation exists in a nation that has such a high percentage of intelligent, educated people? Sum up your thoughts in a short essay.

3

Is advertising in America generally a force for the good or not? Explain and defend as well as you can in logical argument the way you feel.

4

Create and write a brochure, TV script, or magazine ad, persuading college students to use or avoid using this book.

5

In what ways do *you* feel the work you have done in this book will be helpful to you in the future? (Note the authors' comments on the last page.) Draw your ideas together into a clear piece of expository writing.

6 PERSUASION PUZZLE

```
A  M  B  I  G  U  I  T  Y  S  O
L  R  I  Z  J  F  N  E  E  Y  I
L  O  G  O  S  A  I  A  A  L  L
M  O  D  U  A  C  M  C  P  L  I
E  G  G  E  M  T  I  H  P  O  N
N  E  V  I  D  E  N  C  E  G  D
L  O  G  I  C  U  N  A  A  I  U
H  E  A  R  F  A  C  T  L  S  C
O  P  I  N  I  O  N  T  E  M  T
R  A  T  I  O  N  A  L  I  O  I
I  N  F  E  R  E  N  C  E  V  V
S  E  E  P  E  R  S  U  A  D  E
```

The words that fit the following clues are hidden in the maze of letters. Some are written horizontally, some vertically from top to bottom, and some diagonally from left to right. The word always appears in a straight line with no letters skipped.

Some words overlap and letters are used more than once, but not all letters are used. Circle and number each correct word. The initial letter of the correct word appears in parentheses after each clue. The words themselves appear on page 189 in this book.

1. Reasoning that seeks to establish general principles or laws by examination of particular cases. The conclusion is probable. (I)

2. Furnishing proof or support. (E)

3. A logical scheme or analysis of an argument, consisting of three propositions: major premise, minor premise, and conclusion. (S)

   Example:
   All arts are difficult to perform.
   Sculpture is an art.
   Therefore, sculpture is difficult to perform.

4. Reasoning that proceeds from general principles to other general principles or to particulars. The conclusion is certain if the premise is. (D)

5. Reasoning designed to convince or persuade. (A)

6. Call for sympathetic response or decision in one's favor. (A)

7. That which has actual existence, or is manifest in experience. (F)

8. What a person thinks or believes about something, a view, a judgment. (O)

9. Sound reasoning or argumentation, rational development. (L)

10. Something which can be understood in two or more senses, equivocal, indefinite, unsettled. (A)

11. To win over by appeal to reason or emotion, to plead, urge, demonstrate. (P)

12. Characterized by reason, intelligent, logical. (R)

13. Truth or proposition drawn from another which is supposed to be true, conclusion from given data or premises. (I)

7

Research and write a term paper on one facet of propaganda used in this country.

8

Go to the library and study the ads in a popular magazine published in Britain or Canada. Then compare the persuasive techniques used in these ads with those employed in a similar magazine published in the United States. Write an essay in which you discuss the impact of your findings.

9

Are there some aspects of education you have received in school that you consider to be a form of propaganda? Have you always accepted what teachers and textbooks tell you, or have you been encouraged to research, weigh evidence, and make up your own mind? Write a paper that explores your answers to these questions. What insights about the process of education has writing this essay given you?

10

Many young people today are embittered and angry about the state of our society. They see that change is necessary. To try to change matters by violence has proven futile. But verbal persuasion levied in the right quarter by a sufficient number of people would have tremendous impact. Change could be effected this way. If there are some facets of our society that seem unsatisfactory to you, list them. Choose one that you feel is particularly urgent and work up a campaign of persuasive letters directed to those who stand in need of your persuasion.

11

You are the wise anthropologist who is an expert on communication of the twentieth century. In the year 2276, you publish an article arguing that the Americans of the period after 1950 established the first "modern" methods of utilizing new media for propaganda purposes. What evidence do you offer to support this thesis?

In honor of the 500th anniversary of the Declaration of Independence, you are asked to write an article describing in detail the modes of persuasion used by the Americans of 1776 and of 1976. What does the article say?

Then, inspired by your essay, one of your collegues undertakes to write a complete description of the propaganda methods of 2276 to compare with those of 300 years earlier.

Your first articles are so successful, you are asked to write another, evaluating the propaganda of the past and recommending which techniques should be revived for use in 2276. You state that most of them should be used by your contemporaries. Why?

An anthropologist in another university responds by writing an article declaring that the propaganda of the 1970's was harmful and dishonest. What are the bases of that opinion?

Finally, you assemble all your studies and those of the other anthropologists into a textbook. What title do you give it?

OVER AND OUT...

We, the authors, believe that your work in this book should have heightened your awareness of the propaganda that continually surrounds you. You ought now to be able to sift doublespeak from honest persuasion so that you can make sound judgments on the basis of what you see, read, and hear. We also feel that you should be able to muster logically argued persuasion on behalf of whatever cause you may believe in—whether it be in school or in society at large.